365 Things
Every *Woman*
Should Know

EMILIE BARNES

HARVEST HOUSE PUBLISHERS

EUGENE, OREGON

Cover photo © Maria Mosolova/Photographer's Choice RF/Getty Images

Cover by Dugan Design Group, Bloomington, Minnesota

365 THINGS EVERY WOMAN SHOULD KNOW
Copyright © 2010 by Emilie Barnes
Published by Harvest House Publishers
Eugene, Oregon 97402
www.harvesthousepublishers.com

ISBN 978-0-7369-2851-9

365 Things
Every Woman Should Know

*K*nowing we're created by God is such amazing knowledge, isn't it? And the gift of our femininity is something we can give to ourselves and everyone around us. The woman's touch in a flower, a candle, a little caring gift can say so much to someone. Celebrate the unique things about your friends. Finding something personal is fun and makes gift-giving more special.

*I*n the 50s women believed in home, children, and prayer. In the 60s it was "do your own thing." The 70s were all about "being liberated." In the 80s it was becoming "superwoman." In the 90s we were tapping at the "glass ceiling." In the first decade of the 2000s, we went "green" and became environmentalists. What's next? *We're exhausted!*

Proverbs 19:8 says, "He who gets wisdom loves his own soul; he who cherishes understanding prospers." So do yourself a favor and learn all you can. I want to be a woman who holds my home and family together like mortar. Don't you? As women, let's change our values from straw and sticks to gold and silver by building a strong foundation of faith in God's Word.

⤸

*O*ne great way to add more hours in your day involves a life principle that has worked for me: "Keep it simple!" The idea is to order your life in a way that gives you time and energy to spend with God and care for others. Why not try it today?

⤸

*H*ow can someone pray constantly? Is that even possible? After all, we're busy moms. But then I battled life-threatening cancer for several years. As a result, I've experienced a new depth and understanding of this thing called prayer.

When your child faces a dangerous illness or when your husband's job is threatened are prime times when we discover that praying without ceasing *is* possible. But we don't need to wait for something bad to happen. Sometimes our prayer needs to simply be "God, please give me the insight to know *who* I am to pray for. Show me what *You* desire for my life. Give me patience to wait for *Your* timing." God answers our prayers. Trust Him and His plan for your life.

~

*L*ower your cleaning expectations if you're feeling overwhelmed. There's a big difference between dirty and messy.

~

A special gift captures a memory. The next time you experience a special occasion— a friend's birthday, a career milestone, a personal achievement—why not write a letter to the friend or friends associated with it? Save the letter and send it when that person needs cheering up or for another special occasion. One mother I know wrote a letter to her newborn that included her hopes and dreams for that child. She's going to mail it on her daughter's eighteenth birthday.

~

*N*othing makes my day like getting a note from an old friend. And I so love getting family pictures. For something a little different this year, why not have your children design the birthday,

5

Christmas, and other cards you send? They're sure to come up with something creative. Make designing, creating, and sending cards a family tradition. Put on some upbeat music and go for it! And have everyone—including Dad—spend an evening writing notes and addressing the cards.

*M*om—you can't do it alone. Humanly speaking, your survival is in three areas:

- *Delegation.* Call a family meeting today and get everyone involved in house upkeep. Your family will come through for you if you give them the chance—and a little prodding.

- *Dialog.* Share your stress. As busy as you are, it's important to communicate your feelings and concerns to your family...and also to God.

- *Interaction.* Work side-by-side with your family when you can. Bake cookies, wash the car, shop together. You'll be amazed at how much sharing you'll get in as you labor together.

*D*on't waste time arguing. A smart woman loves the man she married, and she lets him know it often. And who's the winner? Both of you!

~

*G*reat women are willing to make positive changes—changes that first come in our relationship with God. Let's be liberated in our homes because we've built a strong foundation on Jesus Christ, our ultimate source of strength, love, forgiveness, peace, and joy. Proverbs 24:3 says, "By wisdom a house is built, and through understanding it is established; through knowledge its rooms are filled with rare and beautiful treasures."

~

*P*arties are wonderful, but you've got to plan ahead. Whether it's a holiday gathering or a special event, get your invitations out early so people can include your celebration in their schedules.

- Decide what kind of party you're going to hold. Plan your menu now so you can buy groceries and decorating supplies.

7

- Get everything together that you want to use for your table decorations.

- Make desserts and as much food as possible ahead of time and store in the freezer.

- Have everything on hand for your favorite drinks (wassail for Christmas, cider for fall, lemonade for summer, ice tea for spring, hot cocoa for winter). Arrange decoratively to your festive display.

- If table linens are a problem, use a full- or queen-size sheet. It's easy and looks great. Add wonderful napkins, some seasonal decorations, a few beautifully scented candles, and—voila!—you're all set to enjoy a delightful celebration with family and friends.

etting organized seems to be everyone's concern. Did you know that it starts with you? Do you have a plan? If you don't, you need one. Write down everything you want to accomplish. Don't rely on your memory. Keep a little notebook with you and jot down things that come to mind. And once you write it down, don't forget to read it later. (Don't laugh. That's where a lot of us drop the ball.) And by all means, keep lists. Believe me, it won't take long before you feel a lot more organized.

~

*W*ant to jazz up your living room? Think designer sheets! You can decorate an entire room at a very low cost. Cover sofas and chairs. Make matching or contrasting designer pillow covers.

Line an antique armoire with sheets and put in shelves, a crystal lamp, your dishes, and special memory pieces.

Your dining table can have a runner in the same print with a centerpiece of flowers in the same colors. Get creative! For the price of four sheets and a little lace here and there, you've got a newly decorated room.

~

A Celebration Menu

*T*his party menu works! For an appetizer, serve sesame-seed chicken wings, a nice brie, and sliced apples. Roasted turkey for an entree is perfect with a side dish of baked tomatoes—the color adds wonders to your table. Make a red Jell-O fruit salad and serve a veggie medley. Top it all off with chocolate pecan mousse and a cookie tray.

Beverages can include your favorite drink recipe along with raspberry punch, coffee, and tea. If you're having more than one party at your house during the season, use the same menu to simplify preparation.

~

*Y*our quiet time is God's gift to you—the most lovely and healing "should" in your life. Make sure you fit it into your schedule.

~

*C*reating beauty out of something ordinary brings joy. Watching a beautiful afghan coming from a basket of yarn or a beat-up old table being transformed via a beautiful stain or paint job gives you satisfaction. Serving brunch on plates you found at a bargain sale or using an heirloom tablecloth you found at a thrift store warms your heart. And ideas don't have to be original. Picking up suggestions from books and magazines stimulates more imagination. When you exercise creativity, you're using the gifts

and talents God gave you. Share your ideas and innovations...that's really a gift of you.

~

*H*aving a terrible, horrible, no good, very
bad day? Bad days are a given so you might
as well accept them. But can you find hope in them?
I think so.

- No matter what, 24 hours from now the
  day will be over.

- Marinate your heart in Scripture and
  prayer.

- Go ahead and gripe a little bit to someone
  who cares.

- Count to 10 before you respond to anyone.

- Give yourself a lot of TLC. Get some exercise, eat well, and rest.

- Ask for help if you need it.

- Ask God, "What do you want me to learn
  from this yucky day?"

~

I don't know about you, but I need little reminders to keep my spirits up.

- Frame a card with your favorite Scripture verse. Hang it next to the kitchen sink or by the computer. When you need encouragement, think about the verse.

- Invest in a new translation of the Bible, and read your favorite verses to see if the different wordings bring new insights.

- Hang a family photo by your sink, and pray for each member in the morning.

- Be on the lookout for ways to obey God by serving others.

- Turn everyday activities into occasions for prayer and thanksgiving. Before you make a telephone call, pray briefly for the person on the other end, and ask God to bless that life through you.

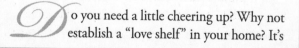

*D*o you need a little cheering up? Why not establish a "love shelf" in your home? It's a great way to display gifts from friends that mean so much but might not fit anywhere else. Then you can look at them and remember people care for you... and you care for people.

~

*D*o something special for you and your loved ones. Surprise your family some evening and eat in a different room for a change of pace. Or if it's warm outside, set up a card table in the back-yard for a special candlelit dinner. A little extra touch here and there can make a lot of difference—even if you're the only one enjoying it. Tie a beautiful rib-bon around your napkin and get some fresh flowers for the table.

~

*W*hy not write love notes to the ones you love? You'll lift their spirits...and yours!

~

*I*f you're running out of space, I can help. I have a friend who lives in a small beach apart-ment, and she has absolutely no wasted space. Here are some of her innovations. She installed a towel rack on the inside of a closet door to hang tablecloths. Her armoire stores her DVD player, CD player, radio, and other accessories. On the top she keeps decorative baskets for storage. She's covered them in bright colors to match her room. She also uses the top of almost everything—refrigerator, cabinets, hutches. She uses her luggage to store items too.

~

I'm a big believer in family traditions. It's never too late to start something new.

- Invent a silent symbol for your family—like a thumbs up, a wink, or a tug on the earlobe—that will draw you immediately closer.

- Tell your children you love them at least once every 24 hours.

- Encourage your children to try new things.

- Have a double-dessert night.

~

*H*ere's a napkin ring idea for a Christmas party. If you have a green, red, and gold plaid tablecloth and solid red napkins, tie it together with gold-painted napkin rings. For cheap and fast napkin rings, cover those empty toilet paper rolls with lace and cut the rolls 2 inches by 3 inches in width. Cookie cutters also make great napkin rings. Let your kids help you come up with unique ideas.

~

*I*f you want to have friends, be friendly. That sounds simple enough, doesn't it? Well sometimes we need a little jump start.

Keep a small supply of business cards with you. It makes it easy to say "Call me" when you meet someone you know or want to know. And if you don't have a "business," make up a personal card you can hand out.

Invite someone to lunch or tea. After your meeting, write down the important things you learn about your new friend: birthday, family members' names, special details.

If someone new moves into your neighborhood or comes to your church, put together a welcome basket. You can include local info, a homemade treat, and something fun. Use your imagination.

Leave room in your life for future friends. Sometimes we schedule ourselves so tightly we miss wonderful opportunities for new things.

~

*S*uccess is a process of realizing worthwhile goals. In the crazy world we live in, we've lost the virtue of patience. So often we steam ahead on our own. Isaiah, God's prophet, said, "I will wait for the LORD." Let's follow his example. Strive for patience, and teach it to your family. It takes 21 days to develop a new habit, so start today.

~

*A*dd some zest to your life and you'll feel better! This past weekend a friend and I spent a couple of hours talking about everything under the sun. Nothing heavy, just "woman talk." It did wonders for both of us.

I encourage you to schedule times with your friends more often. They're more important than you might think.

~

*Q*uiz time! Don't panic, this is just a little test. When you have a minute, I want you to write down six things you like about yourself. Do I hear you "hum and haw"? What happens to so many of us is that over the years our parents, brothers, sisters, and even teachers have put us down. So today it's often hard for us to come up with even six things we like. Let's make sure we change that for *our* children and grandchildren. When your kids and grandkids do something well, be sure to compliment them.

~

*M*ake baking a fun family tradition. I can already smell gingerbread cookies comin' out of the oven. I love to have my grandchildren help me bake. Like with my kids before them, it's a time to talk, listen to festive music, and be together. It makes a hectic week more relaxed. My grandchildren help with the gingerbread cut-outs, the powdered sugar, the fun sprinkles—both on the cookies and on *me*. They love this tradition, and they're always so proud of their creations.

~

*D*id you know that most people are interrupted at least once every five minutes? Interruptions can be real time wasters. My Bob used to waste time looking for his car keys and glasses. One day I put up a key hook by the phone in the kitchen and told him to put his car keys on the hook and his glasses on the counter underneath. Done deal—no more problem!

~

*I*f your kids turn out to be slobs...guess who's going to get the credit? I have a friend who never made her bed. Not only that, everything around her was in disarray. Now she has a son who is 20 years old, and he's an absolute slob. Excuse me, but that's the best way to describe him. And I'm not speaking of just straightening a room. He's chosen a lifestyle of sloppy behavior and sloppy habits. Mom never taught him to take care of himself or his surroundings. Being a mother isn't a popularity contest. Be the mom God wants you to be. Sometimes that means saying, "Make your bed!"

~

*I*f you've got a hectic schedule, break up the tasks into time slots—and stick to it.

~

*T*here are some things that can only be accomplished by meeting with the Lord in quiet. This is when you can get a handle on the many challenging parts of your life. Emotions, worries, and tensions; fears and insecurities; hopes and dreams can be worked through.

During these special moments with God you can get things settled. Maybe that's why Paul advised the Thessalonians, "Make it your ambition to lead a quiet life...so that your daily life may win the respect of outsiders and so that you will not be dependent on anybody" (1 Thessalonians 4:11-12).

~

*Y*ou spend a lot of hours in the kitchen so why not make it a great place to be? First, streamline your kitchen. Eliminate the outdated stuff you don't like or use. Make a list of new items you'd like to have. Put them on your birthday or Christmas list.

A fresh paint job, new knobs on the doors, and

sometimes rearranging items does wonders. When I need more prep space, I throw my breadboard on the stovetop and use it to grate or chop veggies.

And why not hang photographs or kitchen-oriented art if you have wall space? In fact, get the family together to make a meal...and have someone snap pictures to make a collage.

~

*A*s crazy as it sounds, spontaneity can require a lot of careful planning. Ironic isn't it? But that's one reason I encourage you to organize your life—to keep on top of that housework. Have a centerpiece you can pull out for last-minute occasions. Keep silk flowers on hand and a supply of candles. Cook ahead. Have backups in the freezer—spaghetti sauce, a tamale pie casserole, frozen piecrust. When you do, you're always ready for a quick tea party or dinner with old friends—or new ones. When you plan for spontaneous hospitality, it's such a gift. Friendships happen through spending time together, so purposely plan to make that happen.

~

*O*ne of our grandchildren asked my Bob, "Papa Bob, are you rich?" His answer was, "Yes...in the Lord." The grandchild persisted, "No, Papa. I mean *really* rich?"

Somewhere in the mix of values, let your children know that whatever riches you have, it's not the biggest priority in life. Instead, teach them to be good stewards of the gifts God has given—and that includes being generous to others in need by the way you use your time and finances.

Security and peace come from your relationship with Christ. When you live in such a way that your children understand riches in heaven are more exciting than riches on earth—you are training them up in the way they should go.

~

*I*f you have the space, fill a living room with separate little groupings. A wing chair over by a little table with a lamp. A gathering of child-sized chairs and toys near the fireplace. Your husband's oversized chair with its oversized hassock in a cozy corner with a magazine rack next to it and a nice floor lamp. Several little tables can hold groups of photos and other conversation pieces.

All your family room really needs is a comfortable space for everyone to sit, and then one or two places more. This idea works in a large home or a tiny apartment. What matters is not the size of the room, but the warmth and welcome it provides for you and your family.

~

*B*ring some family fun into your home! Choose one day a year for a special family time. Look through photo albums, watch home videos, and reminisce together. Let down your hair and play kid games such as hide and seek. Have a fiesta dinner with all the trimmings. Brighten a wall with a lot of fun family photos.

Have family members keep a list of blessings throughout the year and share them on this special day.

~

*I*f you're at home when your husband arrives from work, be ready. Drop everything and go to greet him. Yes, that's what I said. You know what it tells him when you run to the door to greet him? He's important to you. He's number one in your life after Jesus. You don't know all that's transpired in his day…the frustrations he's encountered. That husband of yours could have gone a hundred different places tonight. There are tons of women out there who would like to have him around, no matter what he looks like or what kind of shape he's in. But he's coming home to you. Enjoy him. Let him know you love him.

~

*I*s your home comfortable? I find it hard to feel comfortable in a house that's dirty, cluttered, or disorganized. I know we're all different in what we can tolerate or like, but I'm convinced that some sense of order is necessary for most people to feel relaxed.

Create a comfortable nest where people you love, including yourself, can work and play and visit. Keep clutter under control and add little touches that make a home feel warm and welcoming.

~

*N*o matter *what* happens keep on praying. If you're feeling overwhelmed with everything you have to do, I want to encourage you. So you haven't gotten everything done…who does, really? But that's okay as long as you're in the process. Keep praying no matter what is going on. When you don't feel like praying, that's when you really need to do it!

⁓

*W*ant to gain a few household stress reducers?

- Color-code the garage key and house key and work key that you search through every morning.

- Sew extra buttons on the inside of your jacket or dress. That way you'll have them if you need them.

- Have a fully equipped emergency kit in the trunk of your car.

- Tape the extra screws that come with furniture to the underside of chairs, sofas, and tables. They'll come in handy someday.

- Write phone numbers, directions, and messages in a notebook you take with you. Or use that Palm Pilot you got for Christmas!

All these time savers are a means to an end—to give you more precious time to spend doing the important things in life.

~

*T*heme gifts can be a wonderful hedge against shopping woes. A friend of mind has decided that this is the year for the "bracelet." She plans to give all of her friends beautiful bracelets picked out with their taste and color preferences in mind—some will be sparkly, others delicate. Everyone loves a special touch of creativity. My bracelet friend? She couldn't bake a cookie if her life depended on it. But if you're one of those people who are masters in the kitchen—oh how your friends will love *your* gift of love from the oven. With those heavenly muffins, add your favorite recipe, put your baked goodies in a cute basket, and you're all set.

~

*W*hat is the first thing you see when you drive up to your house? What catches your eye? What do you like? What are the distractions? What can you do to make your home look more inviting?

Why not choose a small area at the front of your house for something green or growing, such as a rose-bush next to the door or a potted plant on the porch.

Decorate the door for the season to add a bit of "Wow!"

Your home says a lot about who you are. Proverbs 24:3 says, "By wisdom a house is built, and through understanding it is established."

~

*I*f it's Christmastime or a birthday…or any-time you receive cards, display them! Get a tack board and stretch plain-colored or festive print fabric over it. Take ribbons that complement the color of the fabric and create a crisscross pattern across the board. Secure everything with colorful thumbtacks. As cards come in, slide them under the ribbons for a friendship display.

~

*R*educe some of that early morning stress by getting things ready the night before. This sounds simple enough, and yet most people run around in the morning trying to find briefcases, getting their lunches packed, and looking for whatever. Lists are lifesavers. Take control of your time. You need as much as you can get for the really important things you want to do.

~

*W*hat's your number one priority? There was a time when my priorities were out of whack. I needed special times with the Lord, but when my children were little, that meant having to get up at five in the morning. Most days I got up and did what it says in Proverbs 16:3: "Commit to the LORD whatever you do, and your plans will succeed." Some days I'd check my to-do calendar and say, "No way!" But then I'd get up early, read God's Word, put my hands on my calendar and say, "Lord, You know what I have to do today. Help me through every moment." And you know what? When I did that I not only got everything done, I usually had time for a nap too!

~

A peaceful family meal together? I know it sounds like something out of the "old days." In this day and age, it's going to take some planning *and* scheduling, but I guarantee it's worth the effort to have dinner together often.

Keep the conversation lively and entertaining so the meal is a positive experience your family members will want to repeat. Give everyone a chance to share about something good that happened in their day...no matter how small or big.

~

*G*et away from *everything* and *everybody!*
I thought that would get your attention. I need time when I can charge my batteries. For me this means a daily quiet time with God and extended periods of spending special time with my Bob. The stillness gives me a chance to look inside and nurture the real me. It keeps me from being frazzled by the world and its stresses.

I want to spend more time alone with God—talking, listening, and just being. I want those things for you too. And spending time with someone you love and who loves you nurtures the heart.

Don't let the enemy wear you so thin you lose your balance or your perspective. Find time to spend with God and loved ones in a way that builds you up and confirms you're loved. This is just as important as sleep, exercise, and food. It's that simple.

~

*U*se "in-between times" to get things done. For example, it takes 15 minutes or less to change the sheets on a bed. So when you're waiting for dinner to finish cooking, to go somewhere, or for something to finish up, make a bed. Planning saves you time. Know what you have to do—and set your priorities.

~

*H*ere's a fun idea! Why not lighten a gathering together load a little by hosting a tea "potluck." It's a great way to widen your circle of friends *and* expand your recipe files. You provide the beautiful setting—and, of course, the tea. Invite each guest to bring a wonderful tea-time treat to share, along with the recipe. Have fun sampling all the goodies. You can also invite someone to play the piano, the guitar, or even do a dramatic reading of some sort.

After the gathering, create a package of recipes and send them to each participant, along with a "thank you for coming" note. Friends are the continuous threads that help hold our lives together.

~

*I*f you have a fireplace, make it the focus of the room. Add plants, a teddy bear collection, or whatever you like to catch the eye. Add homey touches with a favorite stuffed toy, a framed picture of yourself with your grandmother. Photos and vacation souvenirs are great to liven up a room.

Slipcovers help you make incredible changes in your decor simply. In winter months, toss an afghan over a sofa or chair. When you're not using afghans or blankets, stack them neatly under a shelf or a table to add texture to a room.

Instead of a lamp table, stack wooden trunks or packing boxes together. These make great tables and provide storage.

~

*I*f you're living in a place that's just not big enough for that huge Christmas tree you'd love to have, get branches of evergreen, balsam, or juniper and use them to outline mirrors, arrange on mantels or windowsills, or decorate tabletops and bookshelves. Add gold or silver balls or showcase your holiday collectibles among the branches, such as snow villages, angels, and Christmas teacups. And don't forget to use plenty of unlit candles in seasonal colors. If you do light them, make sure the branches are arranged so they're not a fire hazard. Add a nativity scene to set the significant tone of the season. Make your home warm and welcoming, overflowing with love and good cheer.

~

*T*hose food shows on TV don't have anything on me! Cooking with your friends—inviting them to sit with you while you prepare a fantastic meal is something I've been doing for years. More often, though, I'll put my friends to work. We all have fun pitching in. I've had some of my best conversations while I was stirring a pot of soup and someone else was tossing a salad. I've also had some of my closest times with my husband in that warm, creative room in our house. Good talk seems to happen naturally in the kitchen. And teamwork is great fun! No one is lonely; no one feels left out. Creativity flourishes as you work together.

~

*Y*our children need to be in the kitchen. They need to learn kitchen skills so when they're on their own they can cook nutritious meals...and eventually teach their own children to be self-sufficient. Teach your kids to measure and stir, read recipes, plan entire meals, and clean up as they go. They're also learning organization, teamwork, and a lot more. You'll also have a lot of fun...and it may even be messy fun at times—a treat for kids.

*N*eed a gift box? Cover shoe boxes with wrapping paper. Fill them with stationery, a glue stick, small scissors, paper clips, marking pens, memo pads, and thank-you notes. You can even add stamps. Any mom, dad, grandparent, or teacher would love such a gift.

*M*y motto is "Always be ready for a party." When party supplies go on sale, I stock up. Colored plates, napkins, streamers, little gifts, even party hats.

And here's a tip. When you buy candles to use later, store them in your freezer. It helps them burn longer and cleaner.

Keep a roll of cookie dough in your freezer, some scone mix in the pantry, and some of those great instant coffees so you'll be ready at any party opportunity. There's nothing like a spontaneous celebration to warm hearts. When you're ready, a party can happen in just a few minutes. You'll be creating memories you and your family and friends will cherish forever.

~

*T*ake an hour or so at a discount card shop or dollar store and load up on all kinds of greeting cards—birthday, anniversary, friends, and pets. Store them in a convenient place and use them as special occasions arise. You'll save a lot of time by having them when you need them.

~

*H*ave a "gift shelf" in your home. Load it up with boxes of stationery, stuffed toys, small items—whatever is useful *and on sale* so when occasions arise, you'll be ready. When grandchildren drop by, let them pick a little gift off your shelf.

~

The Bible says, "Submit to one another out of reverence for Christ" (Ephesians 5:21). The Bible also says we're to live in harmony and love. Here are a few thoughts to contemplate.

- A good marriage is not a gift; it's an achievement by God's grace.

- Marriage is not for children; it takes guts and maturity.

- Marriage is tested daily by the ability to compromise.

- Being a family means giving, and—more importantly—forgiving.

- It's time for parents to take charge of their families and redeem them for the Lord.

- If our country is to be strong, our families must be strong.

Today so many children aren't involved in their families' lives. Let's change that! Get them active in your family. Start by creating times for sharing and conversation…at the dinner table. Turn off the TV, all phones (including cells), and any other distractions. Toward the end of the meal, ask everyone this question: "What's the best thing that happened to you today?" Make dinnertime fun. Find out what's happening in your children's hearts and lives, and let them know what's happening in yours. Honor jobs well done, good grades, and positive contributions to the family and community.

⁓

I love having family pictures all over the house. It's a great way to promote family identity. Do team sports together. Have a family night out every now and then. The apostle Paul says, "If you have any encouragement from being united with Christ…then make my joy complete by being like-minded, having the same love, being one in spirit and purpose" (Philippians 2:1-2).

⁓

*W*hen was the last time you did something really special to say "I love you" to your husband or boyfriend?

In the morning, tell your husband, "Honey, tonight is a special evening—just for the two of us."

Then get busy. Set up a card table on your patio or

deck—or even in the living room. Get out a beautiful tablecloth, your best napkins, flowers, and candles! Fix him his favorite meal and your best dessert, put on some soft romantic music, give yourself enough time to look your best, and you're all set for when he gets home. He'll feel like a king and know he's a top priority in your life.

riendship is a treasure. If you possess even one nugget of the real thing—you're rich! So celebrate! Give your friend a book or an item with a note explaining its importance. Or set up a spa day.

Why not add to her collection—or even start one for her! A bell, a miniature animal, an antique...something in line with her interests. Personalized notepads are always great and practical!

You could get her a monogrammed Bible or a hymnbook for her devotional times. Or one of those wonderful little rosebush trees if she's into gardening.

Express your care and love for her friendship.

hy not widen your circle of friends? Don't miss the joy of sharing your Christian life through hospitality. Bible studies and small-group meetings are great ways to open your home and your heart. Fill a basket with food and take it to neighbors. What a surprise it will be for them!

Host a neighborhood barbecue, potluck, theme dinner (ask everyone to bring something related to the theme), or even start a dinner club and meet somewhere different each month.

Throw an "all girls" party for you and your friends.

Volunteer at a homeless shelter or hospital.

What do you enjoy most? Let that be the focus of your hospitality to others.

*L*aughter is such great medicine. So first of all, don't take life too seriously. There's so much to laugh about. In fact, look for the "sillies" in your circumstances. And laughter is contagious! One time our kids were telling a silly story. What they said set me off, and I started laughing and couldn't stop. No one knew what I was laughing about, but everyone joined in anyway. Make room for laughter in your life. Deliberately seek it out. Proverbs 15:15 says, "The cheerful heart has a continual feast." Be sure to smile today at someone. Find something worth laughing about and go for it big time.

*W*hy not make a few healthy resolutions?

- Don't let children watch TV or play video games on school nights.

- Don't let feelings of inadequacy creep up on you because your kids aren't doing well in school. Encourage them and do what has to be done to correct the problems. Be available to help with homework, but realize ultimately homework is their responsibility.

- Don't bail your children out when they leave their books at home. A couple of times of forgetting and doing without and you'd be surprised how their memories will improve.

- Support your child's teacher. If there is a problem with a teacher, talk it over with your child and the teacher, together or separately, as appropriate.

- Help your children grow and excel in the

gifts God has given them. Let them know you're on their team.

~

*Y*ou spend a lot of time in your home, so make it a joyful place conducive to prayer. Turn on some Christian music and get the celebration of your life in Christ going! Let the music flow into your heart because of the love of Jesus Christ. Psalm 118:24 says, "This is the day the LORD has made; let us rejoice and be glad in it."

~

*A*s a mom I want to leave a legacy that goes way beyond ordinary life skills such as cooking and cleaning. I want to teach values about caring for ourselves and others and shaping a godly atmosphere at home and in our lives.

The time you spend teaching your daughters the joys and responsibilities of womanhood will benefit generations to come. And we teach best by what we are, don't we? Not by what we say. And how we raise our sons demonstrates how they should treat the women they encounter: teachers, moms, their wives, and daughters. My prayer is, "Lord, may Your love permeate my heart and life. May the gentle but strong spirit of being a woman of Yours add beauty and meaning to generations to come. Amen."

~

on't you love springtime? It's a time for planting, for growing, for awakening. There's no better place to be than your garden. My first garden was nothing more than a sweet potato in a jar. Remember those? And flowers! They're food to my soul. My mama would always pick a few to float in a bowl or gather in a jelly jar. And once in a while we'd splurge and spend precious money on daisies or carnations from a florist. Remember the old hymn with the line, "I come to the garden alone"? If I want to get away and be with my Lord, a garden's my first choice. Take some time today to…what is it they say?…Yes! To smell the roses.

~

e live in a day and age where manners have been all but forgotten. We can remedy that with our children and grandchildren. When teaching the "M" word, show your children manners can be fun.

One way is to have interesting pretend conversations that teach saying "hello," "goodbye," "I'm happy to meet you," and "thank you very much." Make a game of teaching kids how to set a table. Knife here. Fork there. Napkin fluffed in a napkin ring—and a pretty bowl of flowers or other decoration in the middle. Make a date with your grandchildren and take them out to lunch so they can practice their skills. Yes, manners can be used even if they're just ordering grilled-cheese sandwiches! Manners will help children have kinder hearts, think of others, and stand them in good stead when they grow up and join the workforce. *Love* has manners, and emphasize how much they're showing they care when they use their good manners.

~

What's the greatest gift we can give to our often impersonal and violent society? Our feminine selves! Does that surprise you? Let me share a few simple truths about being a woman of God. Women have always had the ability to transform their surroundings, to make them more comfortable and inviting so friends can find comfort and joy. Let's rejoice in this gift and make the most of it.

The beautiful woman is disciplined, modest,

discreet, gracious, self-controlled, and organized. Scripture says that as women our worth is far above jewels. Strength and dignity are our clothing. When we open our mouths, wisdom and the teaching of kindness are on our tongues. We are women who fear the Lord. Let's live up to that description and celebrate who we are in Christ.

Have you noticed the focus these days is back on the simple things of life? What's the first thing you do when you pick a rose? You smell the fragrance. Maybe it brings back a memory of the time you picked flowers for your mom. Perhaps it's time to recapture some of that girlhood simplicity.

A lavender sachet in your drawer can be an unexpected and simple pleasure. Spray a little cologne on your notepaper or even on the bathroom throw rug. Or better yet, boil a little pot of cinnamon and enjoy the aroma. Put on lively music while you do your housework. Light candles for a quiet yet festive atmosphere. When we find satisfaction in the little things in life, we are happier and more willing to look for the positive in bigger things.

*C*olor in your home can make a world of difference. It can help you redefine spaces. If an area is too large, add a throw rug in a complementary color and create a "get together" spot. Add some soft-colored curtains for a change of seasons. The idea is to create intimacy, a place that's inviting on a chilly evening or a warm spring afternoon. The richer the colors, the more welcoming the space. Red is great for warmth. Go for it! And shades of cranberry and plum work well. Experiment and step out of your comfort zone. Your home can be a place that gives you a feeling of quiet for thinking about what really counts in life and also be a festive atmosphere for celebrating.

*D*on't put all your emotional eggs in one basket. Our work consumes much of our time, and that's natural. And for some of you, that's 95 percent of your awake hours. Is it time to change your focus—to make life a little easier and less stressful for your family and you? Before you break out in hives just thinking about cutting back—let me give you a few withdrawal tips.

Is there a hobby you've always wanted to pursue? Why not do it now? Learn new things. Volunteer at your church or in your community. Have you always wanted to play the piano? Take lessons! By committing some of your time to pursuits other than work, you'll also discover more energy, enthusiasm, and more areas where God can use you.

~

I love to have pillows everywhere. They warm up a room so easily and without a lot of expense. I've discovered oversized pillows are a lot more comfortable than smaller ones. Make sure some of your pillows are filled with down. They're much more comfortable. (But know which ones they are in case some of your guests are allergic to down.) You can even have old ones restuffed. And don't be afraid to mix the patterns. Florals, stripes, bold colors—as long as they're in your color scheme go for it in every room. You'll be amazed at the transformation. Make your home the kind of place you and your family want to spend time in.

~

*C*lear some time in your week for creative pursuits, whether it's writing poetry, performing music, or planting a garden. Most of all, open your heart and let God fill you with His love and His creativity. He wants to nurture you, care for you, and help you grow.

~

*S*ay cheese!" If you're like most women I know, you have at least one family and friends photo area in your home. My entire home is practically a photo gallery! Walls, tabletops, and my refrigerator door are all crowded with the faces of people I love. My husband, Bob, my children, grandchildren, new friends, old friends—you name 'em and I've displayed 'em. How precious are these gatherings of faces to us. And it's so fitting, isn't it? Because our family and friends' pictures tell the story of their lives...and ours! Cherish your family and friends and those priceless moments. Hold them close. Seek out your friends and enjoy their company more often. Treasure their faces, their characteristics, their uniqueness. But also make room for new people...and add them to the gallery in your heart.

~

*W*ant to hold a spring garden party? It can be a birthday, a graduation, or just a celebration. For invitations, glue inexpensive packets of seeds to index cards and write in your party information. Pass them out or stick them in envelopes and mail them.

Decorate a picnic table with an umbrella and bright floral sheets or vinyl cloths. Why not decorate the awnings and porch posts to make it even more festive? Flowers, flowers, and flowers everywhere create a bright, aromatic space.

If you're limber and energetic or you're inviting kids, spread sheets on the ground for an authentic, old-fashioned picnic. A little red wagon or painted tub with a potted plant makes a fun off-to-the-side "centerpiece." Use a clean watering can for your lemonade pitcher. Engage your imagination and have fun entertaining.

Spring is a great time to introduce your children to the wonders of God's creation. Take them to a garden center and let them pick out a tree to be planted in your yard. Let them help dig the hole, add soil amendments, and place the tree. As they fill the hole around the tree, talk about how amazing God was when creating the world. Your children will love watching the tree grow through the years…as they grow with it.

And remember when you used to press flowers in a scrapbook? Why not do it again? Use the pages of your phone book or apply heavy weight as you press and dry the flowers. When they're completely dry, use a tiny bit of glue to arrange them on colorful or white poster board. Add lace and ribbon, and you've got a perfect pressed flower arrangement. Or make it more masculine by adding graphics of sports, animals, cars, or trucks.

~

*H*ere's a tip that'll help in the dilemma of what to do with your various collections. Always arrange them in odd-numbered groupings. Three is a magic number. Cluster things that have differing shapes, but keep a theme going.

~

*W*ho is your best friend? Who is your second best friend? Now think about it. Is there really such a thing as a "bad" friend? Not all friendships are alike, to be sure. Some are casual and relaxing. Others are intense and stimulating. And some surprise us by seeming to come out of nowhere. Some friendships will fade...a truth we have to accept.

I have several "friends of the heart." These people aren't necessarily "best friends" because they don't need to be that exclusive. Although, come to think about it, there is something warm and wonderful about the words "best friends." "Friends of the heart" are chosen sisters. The ones who make us wonder what we did to deserve them. And best of all, they feel the same way about us. Nurture and cherish those special friendships.

~

*W*ant to give a memorable tea party? Want a wonderful moment to share God's love? For my granddaughters and their friends I carefully selected old teacups—all different and lovely. Then I put out clean hankies to use as napkins, along with spoons for each girl. We had special tea treats and a lovely time.

Once we'd had our delightful tea, we collected all the cups and carefully washed them together. As I handed a cup back to each girl to take home, I said, "The teacup you hold in your hand is beautiful, just as you are in God's sight. Look closely at your teacup. Do you see a chip or crack? That's okay. Life brings cracks and chips, but the teacup is still beautiful and can still be used. And even though you may get a bit chipped and cracked here and there, you're still beautiful and useful to God. He loves you! Remember this every time you look at this cup."

~

*H*ave family photographs copied at your local camera shop and give copies as gifts. Take your children on a memory journey—visit and talk about the places you frequented as a child.

~

*T*hank you." These two magic words are perhaps the most neglected in our vocabulary. When I thank someone for doing something nice for me—sending me a present, cooking dinner for me, or doing me a special favor, they feel appreciated. There's something special about hand-written notes. For one thing, the recipient can read them over and over again, enjoying the friendship represented and the sentiment.

The flip side is that saying "thank you" also makes me feel better. It reminds me of the nice thing the other person did for me.

~

*M*y friend, you don't have to travel life alone. I don't know what your personal journey has been or what earthquakes are shaking your foundations. I don't know what worries keep you up at night, what pains sap your strength, or what drags down your spirit. But no matter what road you're traveling, I do know the Lord is beside you every step of the way. Sometimes you'll see Him when you look back at your path and see what He's been doing. When you suffer, He'll wrap you in His arms. When your strength gives out, He'll carry you or give you strength. And when the ground beneath you seems to give way, He will steady your feet and put you on solid ground. God is with you!

*W*ake up and smell the roses!" I love a garden, don't you? What a relief to have a place where the trees and plants clean and refresh the air. A garden is also a place where I can feel content and even carefree. It's a wonderful relief from places where I hear bad news, noisy traffic, and the hustle and bustle of life. In the garden I'm renewed. I know I can't stay out here all day. There's work to be done. But in this moment, at this time, I'm free to commune quietly with God.

God speaks to me here. My senses rejoice and wonder is awakened.

~

*W*hy not use your cherished collectibles in unconventional ways? That old doorstop you inherited from Grandma? Put it on a side table. If you want a nice, rosy glow in your room, use pink light bulbs. Fill some of those spaces with old books. Buy pictures based on a theme you like and go with it. Reflections from old mirrors or glass, even if they're slightly distorted, give a room warmth and interest. One of my friends even "antiqued" a new mirror and put it in an old frame. Use a mirror as a tray for your candles. There are wonderful, innovative things you can do if you let your creative juices flow.

~

*W*hen everything's new and you want more of a lived-in feeling, one decorator suggests you "age the room." What does he mean by that? For one thing, use vintage pieces to give a sense of charm, a different era feel. This will make your home look less "manufactured." Oil paintings, leather books, a family Bible (old or new), and your favorite collections all add to the "we've lived here for a while" feeling.

~

*O*ne of the simplest ways to save money is to delay gratification. Okay, I know I may have shocked some of you. But this principle is a key to financial maturity. When you're about to make an impulse purchase, delay it. Put it off for 24 hours… or even an hour if that's all you can handle. Giving yourself time to think helps you truly evaluate whether you want to make that purchase.

And if you're an impulse buyer, why not take a friend with you when you go shopping? Let him or her know your tendencies so they can help strengthen your resolve to think before buying.

~

*W*ant to hold a garage sale? It's a great way to acquire money and get rid of clutter and unwanted items. First clean the house and decide what to sell. Spend time with each child so you can discuss what they want to contribute. Sometimes in the enthusiasm of getting money they want to sell their beds…and even the dog or cat. And don't get carried away yourself. Once I got so excited that I sold our refrigerator!

~

*W*ith birthday parties coming around all the time, is there a way to simplify gift giving? You bet. And you don't need to spend a lot of time or money if you plan ahead.

- Look into getting a poster of your child's favorite hero or pastimes.

- A supply of 10 "coupons" that excuse your child from one chore a day is a much-appreciated gift. Make sure you put "Only one coupon may be redeemed per day" on them.

- A certificate of promise for your child to have a slumber party or a special outing is great, but remember to follow through.

- For older teens, a 5- or 10-hole punch card for using the family vehicle is popular.

Keeping it simple and personal shows gift receivers that you've put some thought into who they are and picked gifts just for them.

~

*H*ow are your priorities? When my children were still at home, I often reminded myself, *Emilie, you were a wife to your husband before you were a mother to your children. The children will grow up and leave—hopefully! But you'll still have your husband.* What was I reminding myself to do? Spend quality time with Bob without the children.

This is such a crucial aspect of married life. Don't find excuses, such as you can't afford hiring a babysitter or going out. You can't afford *not* to. Be creative and find a way. Bob and I planned times together and put them on our calendars just like other appointments. Yes, you may have to leave some things undone, and your children may even complain a bit. But don't let those things stop you.

*W*hy not hold a cookie-baking day with your children, grandchildren, or Bible-study class? You'll have a wonderful time growing closer as you work together.

Bake and decorate cookies and then put them on colorful paper plates. Wrap them in clear cellophane. All you need is a colorful bow and the cookies are ready to deliver to elderly people and neighbors you don't see often.

~

*T*ime can be your friend if you make it work for you. What do I mean? Many of us waste time because we don't have clear direction for our days...or even our lives. Have you ever sat down and written out your life purpose? You may be surprised at what you discover!

It's difficult to choose the best use of our time if we're not sure what we want to accomplish. I have a friend who was approaching the big 5-0. She decided that from that point on, her personal time would be devoted to helping abused children. Because of her goal, decisions about how to use her time became easier because she had focus and knew what she wanted to prepare for. Successful people know how to use their allotted time as a friend. Why not start today?

~

*W*rite to-do lists or thank-you notes during times when you're waiting at the car wash or the dentist's office.

~

*H*ave you ever thought of your life as a pantry? I encourage you to stock your "pantry" with knowledge of the Father, the Son, and the Holy Spirit. For long periods during my difficult and painful cancer years, my eyes wouldn't focus well so I couldn't read. Thankfully, I had spent many years hiding God's Word in my heart and studying His principles. So on my many sleepless nights, I could go to my Scripture pantry and retrieve spiritual help and hope. And on afternoons when I was barely awake because of medication, my Bob would read to me from the book of Psalms. And since I was familiar with many of them, they made it through my mental haze and gave me comfort.

My years of prayer, years of trusting God, years of getting to know Him on an intimate level, and years of setting aside at least "15 minutes a day" for prayer had filled my pantry with a large variety of amazing nourishment and special treats.

Do you need to do some "shopping" and stock your pantry?

*A*s much as I believe in taking care of me, I know that if I put all my energy into looking good I've missed the point. The true beauty of who I am comes from within. If that God-given beauty is lacking, no exercise program, eating plan, wardrobe makeover, or spa treatment can put it there. No interior decorating scheme can give it to me. Ruffles and perfumes, jewelry and quality clothes are no substitute for the beauty I have in Christ. That comes from the heart. I nurture it when I pay attention to what's truly important in life. First Peter 3:3 says my beauty should *not* come from outward adornment. Instead, it simply comes from my inner self—my quiet spirit that comes from my Lord and Savior.

Where is your beauty coming from?

⁓

I heard a great Christmas card story. Just for fun, a couple sent Christmas cards to people they didn't know, chosen out of the phone book. They signed them warmly as if they knew the people. And, amazingly, the following year they received many cards from those people. I'm not sure what to make of this...perhaps it's a good way to meet people and spread Christmas cheer?

⁓

*A*dd some festive touches to your life. When you're serving a luncheon or having friends over for tea, a white tablecloth makes a great background for colorful touches. Sprinkle confetti or multicolored flower petals down the center. Instead of matching your napkins, use a different color for each one. Fluff them like flowers in a basket or in a vase or even in a teacup. For your centerpiece, use a low dish with an arrangement of an assortment of flowers in a variety of colors.

~

I want to be someone who really celebrates the gift of the people God has given me to love. Here are a few simple ways to celebrate friends.

Hold a special tea for your friends and their mothers. Celebrate with a tea for graduates, Mother's Day, or the first day of spring. Put on a birthday tea with special attention on the "big 0" ones. The anniversary of a special event or even a cup of tea to celebrate the end of a bad week or month are also good reasons to commune together.

~

*T*oday why not do a spontaneous act of kindness? Write a note to someone who would never expect it. Put a rose in your hubby's briefcase. Return a shopping cart for someone. Let someone merge into traffic and give him or her a big wave and smile. A thank-you note out of the blue to someone who's said something nice about you will bless his or her day. Give another driver your parking spot. Leave a gift of money for someone anonymously. Call your mom or dad for no special reason. Send a letter to a teacher and thank him or her for all they do. Ask an older person to tell you his or her life story. Hebrews 13:2 reminds us to "entertain strangers, for by so doing some people have entertained angels without knowing it."

*W*ant to spruce up your bathroom? Don't hesitate to hang pictures in there. Plaques, posters, framed magazine covers—whatever strikes your fancy. Mirrors and clocks are naturals too. Flowers are always a plus. Seashells are also at home in the bathroom. Put them in a bowl, hang them, or glue them to a frame. Add favorite bathroom accessories such as lamps and scented candles. Potpourri gives everything a special ambience. Put in a few unexpected touches to make your bathroom unique.

～

*Y*ou know the old saying "Where there's life, there's hope"? I put it a little differently: "Without hope, life as we know it is impossible." How can we survive without at least a tiny spark of promise? A possibility of moving forward? That's what hope really is, after all. When our lives crash and burn, we need hope as a lifeline.

A guaranteed hope-producer is spending time with children. Get down on the floor and talk to them. And listen to them. Let their youth and enthusiasm rub off on you. And here's the best tip of all, taken from Psalm 39:7: "But now, Lord, what do I look for? My hope is in you." May the God of hope fill you with all joy and peace as you trust in Him.

～

*H*ey, if little things can drag you down, then little things can also pick you up! Here are a few ideas.

- Always keep something green in a little vase or pot by your kitchen sink. And I'm not talking about cash—I'm talking plants.

- Find a small gift book that lifts your spirits and take a moment to read it.

- Schedule lunch with a friend.

- Volunteer at a hospital nursery.

- Write favorite Scripture promises on sticky notes and post them on your bathroom mirror.

- Find a lovely place where you can walk to boost your spirits.

*W*ant an easy and wonderful tradition for you and your children that will provide years of joy? Create a prayer page for each of your family members—husband, children, grandchildren, friends of the heart, and keep them in a notebook. I asked each of the special people in my life to trace his or her handprint on a white sheet of paper. Then I encouraged them, especially the children, to decorate their pages.

When I pray for these people, I put my hand on top of their handprints. These handprints are great visual aids. I know the power of prayer doesn't depend on handprints, but they unite the other person and me in a special way.

~

*I*f you're going to complain, do it creatively. You heard me right. Read the psalms and use them for comfort...but also think of them as an outlet for your feelings. Read them aloud like they are your own words. Get a journal and pour out your feelings on paper. Start your entry with "Dear God" and go from there. If you're musical, try singing the blues to God. That's what spirituals are all about. Invite God along on a walk and pour out your troubles to Him. (And the walking is good for you too.) Ask a trusted friend if you can complain to her. Choose that friend carefully and don't overdo it. Thank God and praise Him for helping you through the situation.

~

A little extra attention to your surroundings can make a big difference in how you feel. What colors lift your spirits? What kind of music makes you feel energetic or peaceful? Do any particular fragrances give you a sense of contentment or remind you of fun times? Are any visual symbols especially meaningful to you? Maybe a flower, the face of a child, and a special book from a friend? Do any scriptures or quotations stick in your mind?

Are you getting the idea? By surrounding yourself with color, music, fragrances, and things that appeal to you, you are lifting your spirit. When hope is all around, it's hard to ignore.

~

*G*et out all those baskets you've stored away and use them as part of your gifts. Fill them with wonderful, fun items. You could create a "bath basket" packed with soaps, shower caps, bubble bath, and bath oil. Or how about a "reading basket" with some of your favorite books, a wonderful devotional, bookmarks, and nameplates? Toys, games, teddy bears, dolls, trucks, puzzles tucked in a big basket are great gifts for kids. Or how about a basket with goodies from the local hardware store? Try a "music basket" for a teenager. The secret is being creative and thinking outside the box...and into a basket!

~

*A*ny room where you work is a room that
needs a dose of joy and motivation. Why do
so many workrooms look gray and drab? Why not get
a bright-red computer? You need function, of course,
but add a little beauty too. Paint your workroom a
bright or soothing color. Hide the clutter in festively
decorated boxes or baskets or behind colorful drapes.
Deck the walls. Have a collage of work-related car-
toons or inspiring quotes. Give everything a facelift.
You'll be surprised at what a difference a beautiful
work space can make in your creativity and produc-
tion. *Caution:* Don't redecorate someone else's work
space without checking with him or her first.

*H*ave you thought of your family photos as a
collection? One of my tables held photos of
many generations of women in our family. I displayed
them in a variety of frames, and the mother-daughter-
granddaughter theme pulled the collection together.
No one could resist stopping and taking a peek. Group
as black-and-white photos or formal or informal in
groups. Another idea is to keep the same frames but
change the photos for the seasons. If you have a ton
of photos, rotate them so you can enjoy your entire

collection. And for a designer touch, add a surprise to your grouping—something that doesn't "match," such as that silly picture of your Aunt Lily. The idea is to share yourself with others in a way that is interesting.

~

*W*ant to change your room? Put two lamps of different sizes on a side table with books, a small clock, a pot of flowers, or a ceramic creation. These change the look and provide better lighting. Your coffee table is an ideal spot for a plant or a terra-cotta pot with candles. For a softer look, add a throw rug made of mohair or wool—something warm and inviting. And I don't know about you, but I like book-shelves in the living room—complete with books, family pictures, and a mixture of the things I collect. I also love to frame favorite scriptures to welcome me as I go from room to room. And what a great reminder of Christ when guests come.

~

*S*tuff. Almost all of us have it in abundance. What can we do with it? One of my favorite hideaways is an old faithful: the cardboard box. Cover it with festive Contact paper and stuff away. Or hang a shelf about a foot from the ceiling, and use it to store items you don't want sitting around. It's also great in a child's room for toys that aren't played with often. Get old school lockers or trunks, paint them, and use them for storage. Clutter around your house can cause clutter in your emotional and spiritual life too, so clean up and spend your best time enjoying life.

~

re you reluctant to share your home with others? Maybe it's not your dream house or you don't have the money right now to decorate the way you'd like to. But you know what? It's not about having a perfect home. It's about your spirit of hospitality, your willingness to share your home and your life with others. Don't wait until everything is perfect because that will never happen. Focus on making your home cozy and comfortable. Your place will always be at its most beautiful when you use it to warm hearts.

~

aking time for your husband doesn't have to be difficult or a hassle. With a little imagination and the desire to make him happy, you can make him feel loved. Are you thinking, *Oh great, now Emilie's telling me what I'm doing wrong with my husband.* Not at all! I just want to give you a few ideas to help you let your husband know he's appreciated.

- When he's within earshot, praise him to a friend or neighbor.

- Thank him for supporting you.

- Tell him how much you love him at least once every day.

- Get tickets for a favorite sporting event.

- Prepare his favorite dinner to celebrate a milestone at work—or just for fun.

We all need respect and devotion. As a wise woman of God, demonstrate these qualities to the man you love.

~

*D*id you know that having everything tidy doesn't always mean you're organized? You can be a neat "clutterer." Instead of asking, "Now, where do I put this?" ask, "Where will I *find* it?" There's a big difference in approach. When your office (or your life for that matter!) is too messy, you can't utilize your time wisely. You spend more time trying to find things than working on the project at hand. What's the clutter costing you? Most likely time, money, and, if you're operating a business, customers. And what message are you passing along to your family?

Remember, being organized is *not* a personality trait. It's a skill you can learn. The secret is to get organized and then maintain it over the long haul. Once you've accomplished that, you can meet the challenges of each new day with energy and enthusiasm.

he psalmist said, "Be still, and know that I am God" (Psalm 46:10). Easier said than done, right? So many women these days say, "I'm just dying for a little peace and quiet. A chance to relax, to think, and to pray. But I just can't seem to manage it." "Stillness" isn't a word many of us use anymore, let alone experience. Yet today we desperately need this sense. We're constantly on the move, stretched to the max with all the hats we wear and all the demands made on our lives. I encourage you to seek out times to rest, plan, regroup, and draw closer to God. And when you do, His wonderful peace will come into your home and life.

When I was a young woman, my life was tilted more outward. As I grow and mature, my life is getting more and more geared toward heaven. I've increased the time I spend alone with God—talking, listening, and just being. I want to experience His love and let it permeate my life. I want those things for you too. In fact, I urge you to do whatever is necessary to nurture God's Spirit in your life. Don't let the enemy (Satan) wear you so thin that you lose balance and perspective. A regular quiet time with God is as important and necessary as sleep or exercise or food.

Have you thought about writing a memoir? When I asked that, did you think, *Oh sure, like I have tons of time to sit around writing about me.* Wait...hear me out. Your life is an important story that'll be lost unless you take the time to preserve it. So pick up a pen, go to the computer, pull out that box of old photos. Write your story the same way you talk. Be sure to include dates and places and feelings. Tell about your loneliness the first time you were away from home. Relate what was happening to you to something taking place in the world. Don't be afraid to say what you think and what you've learned. Read other biographies for ideas. And best of all, share what God has meant to you, and what He's done in your life. That's a story your children and their children and their children's children need to hear.

~

As a mom who loves the Lord, you don't have to prove yourself to anyone. A godly woman, you have inner peace. You're strong, yet you don't use your strength to control others. You have that inner contentment that comes from an awareness of God's love in your life. I remember a 92-year-old woman who attended one of my seminars. She took notes through all four sessions. I thought, *At 92, who even cares?* But she told me she wanted to learn everything she could in life so she could pass it on to younger women. You better believe that humbled and blessed me! I hope when I'm that age I'm just as eager to learn and grow in God's grace. As women we can do almost anything, but the point is not what we do but whose we are.

~

When I was 26, our little family moved to Newport Beach, California. It's a beautiful beach town with wonderful people. But to me, the most enchanting aspects were the four older women who took me under their wings. They drew me into a Tuesday-morning prayer group. For four years I sat with those women who took God's Word and implemented it in their lives. I remember thinking, *That's the kind of woman I want to be.* These many years later, those four friends are still drawing younger women into their group—teaching them, loving them, and modeling a spirit of godliness. What a wonderful heritage! And you can give your daughters and other younger women the same heritage. Why not start today?

The average person wastes 2½ hours every day. If we had that time in a single block of time, wouldn't that be great? Unfortunately the time usually comes in 5- to 10-minute segments. But even in those few minutes you can get a lot done. The key is to find small tasks or be willing to make a dent in a large one.

You can file your nails, make appointments, clean a shelf, throw in a load of laundry, or write a thank-you note. One pastor gave a copy of the book of Psalms to everyone in his congregation. He suggests they use it when they have a minute or so of "waiting" time. Why not make a list of what you can accomplish in five minutes so you'll be ready the next time you have a little spare time?

*W*ant some quick reminders to get more out of life?

- In your Bible underline verses that remind you of how much you're loved by God. Check back when you need to be reminded.

- Mend a broken relationship. Don't hesitate to say you're sorry.

- Hang around with loving, giving people. Their attitude and joy are contagious. And we need all the love we can get, don't we?

- Practice delight! The more you notice and rejoice in what God has done, the more positive and loving you'll feel.

*B*e spontaneous and throw a party. You can make just about any occasion special. Now don't laugh, but being spontaneous sometimes takes a little planning. For instance, you'll want to have something fun to eat in the freezer that you can prepare quickly. Have a nice flower centerpiece tucked away somewhere. And candles—who doesn't have candles stashed in a drawer? A supply of party napkins, plates, and plastic dinnerware is great to have on hand.

Because I was once a little girl who never had a tea party, I never tire of throwing one for the people I love. And it doesn't take much to inspire me. A good report card, an old friend in town, a project completed, a promotion—whatever the reason, I'm ready! These are times that say to family and friends, "I have time for you. You are special in my life. Let's celebrate together!"

*D*on't you just love opening presents? I do! And I love giving gifts to my family and friends. I keep a gift drawer full of special little items that caught my eye. Whenever I go "treasure hunting," I pick up a few special things for the drawer. A pretty dessert plate from an antique store (later it may hold cookies or brownies covered with pretty cellophane and tied with a special gift ribbon) or a fun tea towel. Then when a birthday or anniversary rolls around, I go "shopping" in my gift drawer. And don't forget time itself can be a wonderful gift.

~

*M*ake family parties a tradition at your house. Why not throw a theme party? One of my family's favorites is a "pig party." Everyone wears pink. We even had mud pie for dessert.

I have a friend who makes just about every meal she serves a party. There's always a little surprise, such as candles, special place-settings, flowers, or eating on the floor in the living room picnic style.

Let your children join in with their creative ideas. Yes, there may be a disaster or two, but who cares? Celebrate what God has done. The next time you eat together, have a "be glad" verse for everyone to read. Now that's a party!

~

*W*hy have a home in the first place? Good question! When I have a tea party for my grandchildren, I'm passing on to them the things my mama passed on to me—the value of manners and the joy of spending quiet time together. When Bob reads a Bible story to those little ones, he's passing along his deep faith. When we watch videos together, play games, work on projects—we're building a chain of memories for the future. These aren't lessons that can be taught in lecture form. They're taught through the way we live. What we teach our children—or any child who shares our lives—they will teach to their children. What we share with our children, they will share with generations to come.

~

*A*friend of mine loves the water, the outdoors, and the California sunshine. She says they're a constant reminder of God's incredible creativity. Do you may have a patio or a deck or a small balcony? Bob and I have never regretted the time and expense of creating outdoor areas to spend time in. And when we sit outside, we enhance our experience with a cool salad of homegrown tomatoes and lettuce, a tall glass of lemonade, and beautiful flowers in a basket. Use this wonderful time to con-template all God is doing in your life.

*B*ecome an answer to prayer!

- Call and encourage someone today.
- Mow a neighbor's lawn.
- Give your spouse a back rub.
- Write a check for a local charity.
- Compliment a coworker.
- Bake a pie for someone.
- Slip a $20 bill into the pocket of a needy friend.
- Laugh out loud often and share your smile generously.
- Buy gift certificates and give them away anonymously.

*C*hildren and gardens go naturally togeth-er. Children are observers, and they learn so much more when they can see what they're learning.

And when Mom or Grandma and kids work together, gardening is a great way to build relationships. There's something about digging and weeding that makes sharing confidences so much easier. And it's a great lesson for kids that work can be meaningful. That it brings tangible rewards—fresh vegetables and beautiful flowers. Best of all, the children help *you* learn too. They freshen your wonder. And when they pass on the learning and wonder to their own children, you've helped start a lasting and living legacy.

Four simple ingredients can make a meal memorable. First, the care you take in setting the table establishes the tone or atmosphere. Second is the food. That always gets a starring role. Keep it simple and everyone will enjoy your efforts. Third is an old-fashioned word but a never outdated concept: "fellowship." A time for you and your family to share your lives. No matter how busy you are, don't give up on the concept of family meals together. It's worth the effort to buck the trend and spend time around the table together. And fourth? Peacefulness. Begin by inviting God to be present and thanking Him for the blessings He's bestowed on everyone at the table. Eating doesn't get better than this!

~

*P*eople will make time for what they want or what they feel is really important. Do you have a special time you spend with the Lord every day? Too busy? Well, could you watch TV 25 percent less? Could you get up 15 minutes earlier? With creativity and God's help, you can make time and space for your relationship with your heavenly Father. Maybe the most obvious way is to schedule it. And it doesn't have to be a large chunk of time…as long as you spend some time with Him. There are some things that can only be accomplished by meeting with the Lord in quiet. First Thessalonians 4:11-12 says, "Make it your ambition to lead a quiet life…so that your daily life may win the respect of outsiders and so that you will not be dependent on anybody." Makes sense, doesn't it!

~

*L*et's review three types of people today.

• A *well-poisoner* is someone who is always

negative. "Everything is bad and tomorrow we die!" They believe life isn't worth living. If you want to get depressed, hang around this type of person.

- A *lawn mower* is satisfied with the status quo. If it was good enough for Grandma, it's good enough for me. Or perhaps, "We've done it this way for 20 years, so why change now?" Yikes! Stay away from this person. He or she hasn't had a new idea or a stimulating thought in years.

- A *life enhancer* is alive and well and carrying out God's will in his or her life. It's exciting being around this person, and you'll feel constantly energized.

Which person best describes you? Do you need to make some changes? If so, what will you do?

$\sim$

$\mathcal{B}$ecoming a woman of God begins by making a personal commitment to Jesus Christ. Only He can give you the fresh start you're looking for. Second Corinthians 5:17 is a great reminder: "If anyone is in Christ...the old has gone, the new has come!" I discovered this true principle for myself as a 16-year-old Jewish girl when I received Christ into my heart. My life changed from that moment on. The years since have certainly been an exciting adventure, and I'm not finished yet! Far from it. Growing in godliness is a lifelong process. God is the One who makes life vibrant, but He requires my cooperation. I must always be willing to change what God wants me to change and learn what He wants to teach me. Simple? Sometimes...but sometimes not. Worth it? Absolutely!

ome of my most wonderful experiences have happened within my family. Jesus said, "Where two or three come together in my name, there I am with them" (Matthew 18:20), and I've certainly felt His presence! I've experienced something special during ordinary times, such as...

- spending time with Bob over breakfast

- tucking a child into bed

- having unexpected conversations with grand-children in the kitchen or garden

- during home Bible studies

- prayer times shared with family and friends

These moments are when we get down to business in our lives—the times of loving and encouraging one another.

~

*G*reet guests by having a welcome basket with goodies they can admire and even take home. Before your guests arrive, take a look around your entryway. What do you see first? Is that what you *want* them to see first? Make that first glimpse welcoming and appealing.

~

*I*f you're looking for sparkle in your life, I've got some great ideas.

- Nothing lifts my spirits more than encouraging scriptures. Try framing a card with your favorite Bible verse and hang it next to where you do your work. Talk about sparkle! And make sure your children have their own Bibles to introduce "sparkle" in their lives.

- Ask a friend to be your prayer partner for a week. Call or e-mail each other with prayer requests and praises. Or walk together and get rid of some pounds while praying. Write prayers that go along with a verse of Scripture.

- Volunteer your home for a Bible study.

Be on the lookout for ways to obey God by serving others. Such simple things, but what joy they can bring.

*W*ant a successful party? Remember to laugh! Don't take yourself too seriously—especially when it's party time. Tell jokes, share funny stories that highlight your own embarrassing moments. Celebrate fun memories. One of our favorite family parties is getting out the old photo albums and making fun of ourselves. Guests love it too if you have them bring some pictures of their own to add to the fun.

*K*now when to say "no" to good things and "yes" for the best.

> Everything I didn't do yesterday
> Added to everything I haven't done today
> Plus everything I won't do tomorrow—
> completely exhausts me!
>
> AUTHOR UNKNOWN

*O*ne of the best compliments you can give a friend is to say, "You're such a kind person!" And what exactly *is* a kind person?

- Kindness is an attitude of the heart.
- A kind person goes out of her way to be nice to someone else.

All through Scripture we're shown God's character, and it's one of kindness. So why not lighten someone's load today and bring him or her joy?

- Offer to help lighten someone's load.
- Open the door for someone.
- Even a bright smile conveys kindness.

The Bible says, "Be kind and compassionate to one another" (Ephesians 4:32). So be a blessing in someone's life today.

~

*O*ur hearts will be found in the vicinity of our treasures." That's so true, isn't it? Over the years, I've asked hundreds of women to tell me the stories of their treasures. I've been treated to some incredible stories, from a loving grandmother to an inherited Bible, from a mysterious, closed-up room to antique furniture. I've learned about collections and great recipes. The stories are all about the special objects or people in our lives that speak to us about love and hope and memories. Listen carefully to these words from Psalm 119:16: "[Lord,] I delight in your decrees; I will not neglect your word." Now *that's* a treasure.

~

I don't know what I'd do without friends. They cry with me, laugh with me—and, for sure—they're the ones who most often "speak truth" (whether I want to hear it or not). There's nothing that makes life better than friends. My advice? Do everything you can to nurture the special people in your life. It sometimes takes extra thought and definitely precious time, but what joy is yours when you do! Every Saturday morning at seven, my friend Sharon spends a very special hour on the phone with her sister. It's the highlight of the week for both of them. They love and support one another, laugh, and share even the most mundane happenings of the week.

Enjoy and treasure your relationships!

~

*A*s a child, I was so shy I once hid in a closet at my own birthday party! But again and again, over the years, God has confronted me with opportunities to step outside of myself to touch others. And you know what? Saying yes to God is always a hopeful endeavor. If someone asked me 40 years ago whether I'd ever write a book or speak in front of a large audience, I'd have told her she was crazy. But that's what my ministry became! And as I've matured in the Lord, my hope has grown too. These days I'm far from a hopeless romantic. I'm not a hope*less* anything. I'm a wide-eyed child of God eagerly waiting to see what He has in mind for me next.

~

hese troubling days are the perfect time to enjoy the company of old and dear friends. You can share your sorrows, rejoice at God's love, and reminisce about good times. Through all life's seasons friends add so much depth and meaning. Don't think you have to fill every minute with activities. Spend time talking, listening, and enjoying companionship. Gather around a table of great food and soak up the warmth of years of friendship. Share a verse of Scripture and a time of prayer. The Bible says, "Be joyful always; pray continually; give thanks in all circumstances, for this is God's will for you in Christ Jesus" (1 Thessalonians 5:16-18).

ver the years I've put together a "This Is Your Life" scrapbook for every one of my children. The books are filled with birth announcements, birthday party pictures, graduation memories—everything imaginable. Report cards, favorite Bible verses, photos of friends, even letters they wrote from camp. My kids have so enjoyed their special books—their own personal history. I love the scripture in Proverbs that says: "The memory of the righteous will be a blessing" (10:7). In an age and time when things move so quickly, cherished memories mean so much.

~

*Y*ou were a wife to your husband before you were a mother to your children. The children will grow up and leave…and then what? About now you may be wanting to slip into something more comfortable, such as denial. My counsel is to start right now spending more quality time with your spouse *without* the children. If that means putting dates on the calendar to make sure it happens, so be it! Recognize the priority of your husband's place in your life (and he needs to do the same with respect to you). So take the initiative and put some spark back in your marriage.

~

*M*y Bob puts a lot of thought into the gifts he chooses for me. I love that. He takes the time to consider what I like, what moves me, and what makes me happy. I know he spends precious hours looking for just the perfect gift.

What kinds of gifts do you get for your husband? Are they thoughtful and special? Why not give him a certificate entitling him to an afternoon of uninterrupted sports watching on TV? Or a coupon for a special evening in…with just the two of you. Include his favorite foods and snacks. Let him know that he is loved by you!

M en are different than women. I'm sure that's no surprise to you. Have you ever asked your husband what he wants for gifts? Just for fun, I asked some of the young fathers I know, "What would you like for Father's Day?" One candidly said, "For you not to ask me that question!" (Chuckle.) Another father offered, "No clothing. And please don't buy me a tool because I know what I need. But," he added, "how about a coupon book for getting out of mowing the lawn or washing the car? Or an even better coupon is one that says, 'Entitles bearer to hear one "I will not talk back" and one "You're right and I'm wrong!"' Yes, I know that's probably not going to happen!" My favorite was, "For my kids to say, 'I want to do something just with you!'"

ome means coziness, being where I belong, nurturing the most important parts of my life, and loving the people most important to me. At the top of that list is my husband, Bob. The world may be a whirlwind of conflict, but with him I'm safe, even peaceful. My favorite days are the ones we spend working side-by-side or planning a special event for our children or grandchildren. Times of praying together for our children and laughing at the antics of our grandchildren are also extremely special. And the tears that we've shared during the challenging moments of being a couple have drawn us so close together.

What does home mean to you? Why not write it down, and then share it with your family?

hristmas is a time to celebrate your heritage in Christ and the traditions of countries around the world. I love the Mexican Christmas tradition of serving a special hot chocolate made with Mexican chocolate comprised of sugar, almonds, and cinnamon. Yummy! The drink is whipped by rolling a wooden stick back and forth in your hand.

Think about your family's roots and the heritages

of the guests you invite to your home this Christmas. Or you can adopt a country, and pray for the children and the families in places that are far less fortunate than ours.

Make these traditions part of your family holidays as you enjoy one another and the sharing that happens when family and friends get together.

~

I'm a "neatnik." My Bob says I'll die with a broom in my hand, and he's right. I love getting my home in order. And as much as Bob teases me, he too thoroughly enjoys our comfortable and clean home. But cleanliness isn't the main point. What I want to do is create a comfortable nest where people I love can work and play and relax without worrying about whether they'll catch cold from an unwashed glass, trip over junk sitting around, or be faced with a pile of dirty clothes.

~

*I*s your house the "in" place to be? What makes it that way? Or how can you make it that way? Try these:

- a guest book for visitors to sign
- flowers at the doorway
- a potted plant on the porch
- a patriotic flag or festive banner hanging on your porch
- create a "welcome bag" with your guest's name on it. If for a child, put in an apple, a pack of gum, crayons, some paper, a little picture book. For an adult, put in tea, cookies, a special Scripture verse, something inexpensive but fun.

~

*D*id you make your bed this morning? No, I'm not your mom. Yes, I'm from a generation that was taught to make their beds every morning. And I do. Frankly, a made-up bed is so much more welcoming at the end of a hard day than a tangle of sheets. The message centers on clutter. A wise person once said, "Clutter wearies the spirit and fights against serenity." These days there's enough clutter of heart and home to last a lifetime. It's so much nicer to "order your day," as the Scripture says. That gives you more time for the really important things God has for you to do. We all need a place where we can rest and relax and refresh ourselves spiritually and physically.

～

*T*he best tip of all is to give thanks to God for all the abundance He's given you. Whether it's in prayers, songs, or as you say grace before your meal, it will bring you closer together as a family and help you remember others in need.

～

*I*f you want a friend, you have to be a friend. It doesn't matter how old or how young you are, making friends is serious business. So get started! And that's pretty good advice, even if I do say so myself. *Someone* has to make the first move. Why not take a class or sign up at a gym? Join a small group Bible study or dinner group at church? And leave a little space in your schedule. If you have every single evening taken up, where's the room for spontaneity and making friends? If you meet someone you'd like to know better, send her an e-mail and make arrangements to meet for lunch or dinner. And keep a "yes" in your heart. The next person you meet may turn out to be a lifelong sister.

～

*B*e honest: How many plastic bags do you have folded together in that kitchen drawer? And what about all those magazines stacked beside your bed? And is there any woman who doesn't have a "fat wardrobe"...and a "thin wardrobe"...just in case? Why hang on to them? Get some boxes and start labeling and storing away the important items you may need to find quickly and easily. Take those clothes you haven't worn in a year or more to a local charity. Let someone use them instead of just keeping them in your closet. Recycle those plastic bags and magazines. You can do it!

～

*A*t a very young stage in life parents and children should talk about where things come from. No, I'm not talking about the "birds and the bees." Children need to be taught to give. They should be aware that all things are given from God, and that God is letting them *borrow* the items for a time. Children can understand the concept that we should return to God what He's so abundantly given to us.

When special projects at church come up, get your children involved. Show them how to give financially and with their time and energy. Early training in this important area is so valuable. Your children will learn to be givers, not takers. And you are their primary model.

~

or many women, "no" is one of the most difficult words to say. If we can't learn to turn down "opportunities," we're going to get overcommitted, which leads to stress and bad moods and hurt feelings...to say nothing of guilt. Matthew 6:33 tells us our first priority: "Seek first [God's] kingdom and his righteousness." When God has first place in our lives, it's a lot easier to decide what to do with our time. When I feel hassled or hurried, it's often because this priority (God) is out of order in my life. Usually I need to adjust my schedule to make sure I return to spending quality time with Him. I need to charge my batteries. When I allow Him to fill my heart, I can relax, be happier, and even get more done.

~

*W*hy do it now? There's always tomorrow." Procrastination may seem fine today, but it's not a very good way to lead your life. I can pretty much guarantee you won't accomplish much. Putting things off until tomorrow is the universal "effectiveness killer." We say things like "I hope" or "I wish." How frustrating and how negative! If this is you, here are some simple tips to get going:

- Make little tasks out of big ones. Hardly anything is really hard if you divide it into small jobs.

- Make a commitment to someone, and ask your friend to hold you accountable.

- Set up rewards for accomplishing tasks.

- Give yourself deadlines.

- Resolve to make every day count.

Be a woman of action. Treat each day as being precious. The truth is, when it's gone, it never comes back.

*W*ant to throw a summer tea party? Start by sending tea bags with the invitations. Add a little note inviting guests to enjoy one tea now and one tea later—at your house. Liven up your party by having each guest bring her favorite teacup. When they arrive, have each guest share about her cup and what it means to her. You'll be surprised at the stories. I have one friend who always brings a delicate cup and saucer left to her by her mother. It's the one she used as a little girl when she and her mamma had tea together. Others will be from wedding sets or family heirlooms. Set your tea table with an old family quilt. The centerpiece can be a hat from Grandma's trunk, a pretty bonnet, or some festive garden flowers. Put some effort and imagination into setting a beautiful table.

How's your ability for creative seeing? It's simple once you get the hang of it. For example, in your bathroom why not use a glassed-in bookcase that holds knickknacks? Use a single chair for a bedside table or a sofa table. Bring the garden furniture into the house…or turn your house furniture into garden furniture. Have fun! And don't be afraid to be a little outrageous. You can always change it if you don't like it.

Almost anything can become a lamp…including

old lamps. A stepladder can hold shelves or display family photos. Any furniture can be painted, refinished, or covered. When we learn to *see* creatively—a whole new world opens up.

~

I've discovered a deep kind of hope that keeps me putting one foot in front of the other. As I struggled with cancer, hope was a will to live, a deep, God-given desire to go forward. That powerful force grew stronger as my body grew weaker. Hope is so much more persistent than emotion. It's more basic than belief. Hope is in my heart and in my bones. It's real. This hope is a person. His name is Jesus Christ. His death and resurrection for me, and His living presence in my life give me determination to survive and serve Him.

In desperate struggles for peace, Jesus is indeed the hope of the world. Scripture says, "[God] has given us new birth into a living hope through the resurrection of Jesus Christ from the dead, and into an inheritance that can never perish, spoil or fade" (1 Peter 1:3-4). Isn't that wonderful!

~

$\mathscr{T}$he time you invest in your family is never wasted. You have the capacity and position to shape memories, shape souls, shape hearts. Tea parties you share with your children and grandchildren, the stories you tell them that they'll pass along to their children, the creative ways you teach them about God and the world—these are what determine what will become of tomorrow. The impact can be far more beautiful than any heirlooms or treasures you might leave behind. The time you give to the ones you love is an investment in hearts and lives. Today is the greatest treasure you own. So hold it close but also share it. Proverbs 8:20 says, "I walk in the way of righteousness, along the paths of justice, bestowing wealth on those who love me and making their treasuries full." We can too.

$\mathscr{B}$e a woman of "being," not just a woman of "doing." I don't know about you, but I have no trouble at all in the "doing" department. But taking time to let God mold me and make me more like Him—that's a different story.

I have an idea. Let's begin by listing ten "being" goals to attain by the end of the year. One of my favorites is my "The Lord Provides" notebook. In this notebook I consistently list everything that's been given to Bob and me...and from whom. It's wonderful to see how the Lord leads others to meet our needs. Also take time for prayer and meditation. You'll never regret it.

~

*I*f holidays tend to be lonely for you, I'm offering a few simple words of encouragement. I've observed that when anyone tries to find happiness in him- or herself, anything he or she finds is like a puff of smoke. True joy comes through a relationship with Jesus. And happiness comes to us as a dividend. When we become involved in something demanding—something outside of ourselves—happiness is a by-product.

Wake up each day and thank Jesus for dying on the cross for you. Then look around and see who you can serve. Jesus said that "whoever wants to save his life will lose it, but whoever loses his life for me will find it" (Matthew 16:25). You are well loved, my friend.

~

*N*ow that I'm a grandma, I see the importance of leaving a legacy for my children...

and for their children. Encourage your kids to get to know their grandparents. Give them conversation guides, such as asking "What has your life been like?" or "How was life different when you were growing up?" The answers will surprise them—and maybe you. Ask Grandma and Grandpa to describe the different places they've lived in, the different houses, the pets they've had. And it would be great fun to visit some of the places talked about. Who were their best friends? What did they like to do? What was their favorite teenage activity? Find out their dreams and the surprises in their lives. Look at family photos together and talk about the people and places in the pictures. These are wonderful times to discover more about the people you love and cherish.

If you're planning to go antique shopping this summer, I've got a few tips. I'm no antiques expert, but I am a great shopper. I don't worry too much about discovering priceless objects. I'm in it for the fun. I do have a few rules, though:

- I buy only what I love. An item has to "call" to me.

- I buy only what I can use. That little teddy bear might look great in a guest room.

- Price: Is it in my budget?

- Do I have a place to put it?

- I can break these rules to buy something for someone I love.

⁓

*S*ummers in our country are wonderful. The delicious aroma of barbecues, Fourth of July parades and fireworks, family picnics, diving into a local swimming hole. Summer life just can't be beat. Thinking of our great country and the people who live here brings to mind Psalm 33:18:

> The eyes of the LORD are on those who fear him, on those whose hope is in his unfailing love, to deliver them from death and keep them alive in famine. We wait in hope for the LORD; he is our help and our shield. In him our hearts rejoice, for we trust in his holy name. May your unfailing love rest upon us, O LORD, even as we put our hope in you.

⁓

*W*hen it comes to serving God, look around and ask, "How can I help?" You're bound to find something to do for Christ. It might be kitchen duty at a local mission, serving on a committee at church, or babysitting for a young mom so she can have a break. Big or ordinary, whatever you do, do it in Jesus' name and for Him. Be assured that He is going to lead you to the tasks He's set aside especially for you.

*L*et me encourage you to use one of those long summer weekends to "untrash" that place where you used to put your car.

- Call a meeting and get everyone's schedule cleared for the day you agree upon.

- Make a list of all the jobs, and break them into "fair" work portions.

- Delegate. Put all the jobs in a jar and have each person draw them until they're gone.

- Use large hooks to hang bicycles and equipment. Other items can be stored in plastic trash cans with lids.

- Plan a garage sale.

- Give extra clothes and tools to a charity.

- Install and fill shelves.

- Clean, stack, pile, and toss.

Cleaning the garage can be dirty business. Celebrate a job well done.

~

*D*oes a "50% off" sign make your heart beat just a bit faster? Then plan ahead. Think about birthdays, anniversaries, and other gift-giving events coming up. Buy now and take advantage of sales. I also shop by phone and online. It's amazing how much money I save by comparison shopping. Plus I get the fun of looking through all the specialty catalogs and buying at my leisure. Nice consignment shops are also wonderful when shopping for clothes.

Maximize the resources you have...while blessing the people you love.

~

*T*ime management isn't just keeping busy— it's finding God's focus for you. The first step in managing time is acknowledging you have it. Yep—it's the same 24 hours in everyone's day. By using small bits of time faithfully, you can accomplish great things.

In Jesus' time, the Hebrews spent their evenings with rest, family fellowship, and study and meditation in God's Word. Jesus said, "Seek first [God's] kingdom and his righteousness" (Matthew 6:33). One way to do this is to devote the evening hours to reflection in Him to prepare yourself for the coming day. Sound impossible? It may be difficult, but you'll reap the benefits. Why not try doing this one evening a week to see what a difference it can make? "Seek *first* God's kingdom."

*Y*oung girls love to play dress-up, and they love to have tea. So plan a party. Gather a group of your favorite young people for this special summer event. A group of three to five is a manageable number. Let your guests help with as much of the preparation as possible. Buy or make pretty cards for invitations. It's great if the children want to create them. Don't over direct their efforts. Let them be their party. Get some old hats, scarves, jewelry, gloves, handbags, and artificial flowers for them to use. Allow at least half an hour before the tea for everyone to dress up. And don't forget the camera. You don't want to miss this priceless memory maker. And here's a simple teatime prayer for the girls: "Dear Lord, may our time together be sweetened by sharing and warmed by Your love."

~

Our son Brad is an excellent potter. I'm always amazed how he can take an ugly ball of clay and form it into a beautiful vase. A lot of times the first molding doesn't come out the way he wants, so he smashes it and forms it back into a ball to start over. Brad knows the end product he wants, and he doesn't quit until he gets it right.

That's the picture I get when I read in the Bible that God is a potter, and that I am clay in His hands. God knows what He's doing. He has a master plan. And the best part? God is molding me into *His* image. I get so much comfort knowing I'm being formed by the Master's hand.

~

*L*et's build a clubhouse!" Do you remember uttering those words in your youth? Ah, those were simpler days, weren't they? Long, warm summers of clubhouses, sharing secrets, building forts, and playing hide-and-seek with friends. Do you recall covering a table with blankets and crawling inside for a safe and cozy tent? That's exactly what Psalm 34 reminds me of: "The angel of the LORD *encamps* around those who fear him, and he delivers them." The word "encampment" means a fortress for protection. That's what the Lord has done for me. I can feel His security, even in my pain and fear. So I stand on this promise: No matter what happens all is well. I believe the Lord will deliver me from any danger in His time and in His way. And He does the same for you. So don't worry. He keeps a close watch over you. He's always standing with you.

*W*hat was your favorite summer vacation? One of mine was a summer trip to Idaho. I'd never seen such natural beauty. The tall mountains, beautiful rivers, and so much green everywhere. In fact, a lot of Idaho looks just as it did hundreds of years ago. We had a great time fishing, hiking, roasting hot dogs, and camping. The writer in me imagined God's creation shouting with joy and clapping its hands (see Isaiah 55:12). Here's a thought: When you're enjoying one of your favorite moments, listen to the sounds of creation around you. Be blessed by how good God is.

*W*hy not create a "Summer Project Box" for your kids or grandkids? Find a sturdy cardboard box—a shoe box, hatbox, or whatever works. Use file folders for dividers. On the dividers list summer projects for the children to explore. Have them suggest some activities too. Encourage creativity. Believe me, they'll be creative in what they come up with. Some of ours?

- A file for favorite sports stars. It had photos, articles from newspapers, and even some autographs.

- Wildflowers pressing to use later for art projects, thank-you notes, or Christmas cards.

- Unusual rocks for collecting and painting.

And let me encourage *you* with a reminder from

Psalm 127:3: "Sons are a heritage from the LORD, children a reward from him."

~

*T*he summer lemonade stand is alive and well in cities all across the country. Pass me a glass while you're at it. When you start hearing, "Mom, I don't have anything to do!" it's time to set up a stand for business. This gives the children something to do, and it is also a great way for them to learn something about running a small business.

Here's another idea. Check out the Vacation Bible School activities at your church. These are terrific times for kids to learn memory verses, sing praise choruses, and get to know other children in the church and neighborhood.

~

*L*ooking for the perfect birthday party for a friend? How about "tea for two"? Prepare for this party just as carefully as you would a tea for ten. Write out a formal or semi-formal invitation to the "Tea for Two" on a pretty card and send it. Give yourself plenty of time to decorate the table and prepare the food. Pick out two "companion" flowers—two roses, two carnations, two daffodils—and arrange them in a vase with ferns or baby's breath. Spread a lovely tea cloth on a table or tray. Light a candle and place a little gift—beautifully wrapped—by your friend's plate. Dress up to make the time festive. Have soft music playing. Tell and show your special friend how much she means to you.

~

*T*ake some time just for you. In the early morning, before the day gets too warm, take your coffee or tea out on the patio. Bring along your Bible and have a wonderful quiet time with God. Or maybe you'd enjoy being creative? Take a class or a workshop and learn something fun. Why not practice the piano, read that book you've had sitting on your nightstand, or invite a good friend for a casual tea? At dinner tonight, add some fresh flowers to your table.

Get out a piece of paper and title it "What I would do if I had time." Brainstorm and come up with some great ideas for today and the future. This is a worthwhile investment, I promise.

~

*C*ount your blessings. This is the simplest way I know to bless your life with joy. I was raised in a Jewish home, so I didn't learn Christian hymns. I was a grownup before I heard this wonderful phrase: "Count your blessings, name them one by one." I love the idea of thinking about numbering blessings—literally calling the name of each one. Whenever I'm down, I list what God has done for me. Before I know it, I've had an attitude adjustment. I'm overwhelmed with thankfulness for all God has given me.

I so recommend the practice of counting blessings. Take a sheet of paper and divide it down the middle. Over one column write "Heavenly Blessings." Over the other write "Human Joys." Fill up your paper with every blessing you can think of.

*G*ive me a bouquet of flowers, and I'm your friend for life. Well, maybe it's not quite that simple, but I do love giving and receiving flowers. In a special way, they brighten my day. In these hectic days and times, we need to be conscious of the little things in life that can make so much of a difference in a person's life: an encouraging note, a call to console a friend who's lost a son or daughter, a specially prepared meal for a family who's having a tough time. I love the TV commercial where the elderly lady walks to her mailbox, certain it will be empty. And there she finds a lovely greeting card sent to her by a neighbor. The love of God reaches out to others through you and me. Why not make someone's day today?

~

I haven't always appreciated the value of stillness. I'm an on-the-go type. But as I mature, I understand more and more the importance of those times of quiet. I need to get away from stress and demands for prayer and, frankly, just rest. Resting includes a daily quiet time with God and my husband, Bob. That's when I look inside and discover the real me. I encourage you to purposefully make yourself *un*available. That's right. *Unavailable* for a short time each day. Make an appointment just for you. First Thessalonians 4:11 says, "Make it your ambition to lead a quiet life, to mind your own business and to work with your hands, just as we told you, so that your daily life may win the respect of outsiders." The times you set aside for the Lord will be refreshing and rejuvenating.

~

*W*ant some simple decorating ideas? Okay! Wondering where to hang your hat? I saw a front door decoration that was made up of a hat and silk flowers. Baseball caps are a great way to express your "family personality." Hang them in your family room where everyone can see them. How about hanging a beautiful retro hat inside an empty frame? Or put hats on decorative pegs in a guest bedroom. Have fun decorating with what you already have! It will liven up the place, and it can be a fun project for you and your children and grandchildren.

*W*e've all heard the adage, "Please be patient. God isn't finished with me yet." And that's so true! God is working in our lives. He never gives up. The world wants us to be beautiful, thin, always in control, witty, and charming. I say "Phooey!" And you can quote me. This is how it works. The more you trust God, the more you'll understand His blessings. More and more, you'll be amazed at what He's done in your life. The fun part? Waiting to see what God's going to do next.

*H*ow content are you? In Hebrews 13:5, Paul says, "Keep your lives free from the love of money and be content with what you have, because God has said, 'Never will I leave you; never will I forsake you.'" How are you doing in the contentment department? It's definitely easier said than done in this day and age. We're not content with our jobs, husbands, children, church, or homes. We don't like our clothes, our bodies, or our hair. Let's face it, we're getting to be a bunch of malcontents just waiting for retirement or the rapture, whichever comes first.

When we're overwhelmed, we can't see new opportunities, challenges, or even how to care for another person. We need to focus on God and His plans. We have a choice: to be content or not. Which will you choose?

I encourage you to listen, listen, listen. There are people all around you who are hurting and need your prayers. But how can you keep track of all the requests? Whether it's in a notebook you carry with you or a Palm Pilot, jot down those requests when you hear them—and God's response. You'll become excited as God answers your prayers! Just remember, they won't all be answered with a yes. People die, couples get divorced, and cancer isn't always cured. But what you'll begin to see is that God is sovereign. He has a master plan for every one of us. Take advantage of the wonderful two-way communication God wants to have with you. As your prayer life grows more disciplined, your life will become more productive.

~

*M*y friend Sheila discovered the perfect solution to her housecleaning dilemma. Drowning in a sea of dust, dirt, and clutter, she was at her wit's end. Her friend, Fran, was feeling her pain, so they decided to pool their talents. Now they take turns cleaning each other's homes...together. One week it's Sheila's house, the next it's Fran's. Together they get a lot accomplished. And the topping on the cake? They get to share each other's company, which makes the time and cleaning go by quickly. And the friendship and caring that's grown between them is far more important now than getting the housework done. Sheila and Fran were nervous at first. It's scary to admit to someone else that you need help keeping your house clean. But they are so pleased with the results.

~

ontemplating climbing a mountain? I know that's not what you expected to hear from me, is it? But the mountain I'm talking about is called *life*. And that's where faith comes in. It's just what we need to keep moving on and moving up. Here are a few tips to help you.

- First of all trust your map—God's Word. Pay attention to its wisdom. Don't forget to pace yourself. You don't have to mature in one day. Remember, you're hiking to the summit.

- Refresh yourself in prayer.

- Look back to where you've been and be grateful for your progress.

- Take care of your equipment—your body, mind, and spirit. They've been issued to you by God, and they'll carry you where you need to be.

ometimes it's the little things that make the biggest impact when you reach out to others. I know of one woman who is so inventive she makes her own cards. If you're fortunate enough to receive one, you'll laugh at what I call her "creative encouragement." She uses stamps, clever pictures, and drawings to bring a smile or a word of praise to the recipient. Or consider setting up a "food pantry" to meet the needs of families. Why not send special goodie boxes for men and women in the military or away at school? One church I know solicits a "wish list" from all their missionaries. The people of that church "stand in line"—a gift assembly line—to make those wishes happen. Be a friend to someone today.

*I*f you want to keep and bless your most cherished friends, you have to spend time and energy. And a little creativity never hurts! Most of the time, a little effort is all that's needed: a phone call or e-mail, a thoughtful present, a silly surprise. And my favorite? A cup of tea together. These are the kinds of things that keep us connected.

*F*riends help friends. To be a helpful friend in need—be around. Offer your physical presence and practical help. Maybe it's answering the phone in a time of loss, doing the laundry, or picking up kids from school. And never underestimate the power of prayer support. Don't let your friend push you away. Be extra tolerant and forgiving during stressful times. Always, always let love be your motivator. Having a friend is a great gift!

ne of the great things about having a daughter is spending time with her. I encourage you to plan fun times with your daughter or granddaughter. It's a legacy you'll never regret. Don't let the days and years pass by without investing in memories that will delight and refresh your mother heart. Read a book together...or a chapter anyway. Pack a lunch and have a picnic, even if your child is an adult now. Go to the spa together and get makeovers. Now that should bring up some interesting discussions! Make a tea date. Have a Bible study together, and pray with each other regularly. Rent a vintage movie and laugh and cry together. Have breakfast together every Friday morning. The important thing is to hang out, enjoying your unique mother/daughter friendship. And, come to think of it, do most of these with your sons and grandsons too.

I encourage you to make this Christmas a season of warmth and light—full of welcome to anyone who stops by. Reward your friends with a hearty dose of friendship and the love of Christ. And if the holidays have kind of gotten away from you, here's a prayer: "Father God, help me pause and relax even with all that needs to be done. Fill me with Your joy and peace so I can share You with others. Amen."

~

J ust think how different life would be with no more tears, no more death, no more crying, no more pain. Hard to imagine, isn't it? Pain and unhappiness are familiar to all of us. I guess that's why God's promises have meant so much to me over the years. Revelation 21:4 says God will wipe away the tears from our eyes. There will be no more death, or sorrow, crying, or pain in heaven. All of that will be gone forever. Don't get me wrong. I'm eager to live out every day on earth that God has planned for me. There are so many wonderful things to do for Him and for those I love. But I also look forward to that heavenly time. I so hope you're there with me.

~

*W*hen the school year approaches in the fall, why not make it simpler by planning ahead? Make up a checklist for what your kids will need this fall. Have your children help with this "inventory"—shoes, socks, T-shirts, skirts, pants, uniforms if required, underwear. Get everything ready now and avoid the rush.

~

*I*s life piling up? When you feel everything's pretty much upside down, the world seems to have very little to offer. Have you noticed that? Oh, there are plenty of options out there, but none of them are satisfying or long lasting. None of them except the Word of God, that is. I'm delighted to tell you that the Bible is full of promises and guarantees! For someone as practical as I am, that's great news. God's words echo in my ears when I read He loves me. When I read I can trust Him. When I read He will rescue me. When I read He is helping me improve. I trust the Lord of the Bible! Do you?

~

*I*t's the thought that counts." You've heard that sage bit of advice, I'm sure. However, I disagree with it. The *evidences* of love count. It doesn't take much to reach out in love to people around you. And the surprise that you made the effort goes a long way. You never know who may need an encouraging word.

Here are a few gift ideas to add to your list. For a special gift, why not purchase a monogrammed Bible or special hymnal? Or deliver a surprise dinner—prepared and ready to eat. A favorite movie CD with an invitation to get together provides entertainment and friendship. Free babysitting is always a welcome present for parents. A simple card of good wishes just for fun will brighten someone's day. Gift certificates are always nice. A phone call to say, "Hey, how did it go last week?" shows you care. And letting someone know you're praying for them is an uplifting encouragement.

W ant to "practice hospitality" more? Invite your neighbors over for a "get to know you" snack or dinner. Host a neighborhood barbecue. For a little different angle on hospitality, volunteer to serve meals at a local mission. Start a "dinner club." Take hospitality "on the road" by filling a basket with food and taking it to someone who needs encouragement. And don't miss the joy of sharing by opening your home for Bible studies, small group meetings, and your youth group at church. Here's one more idea, perhaps the best of all: Share hospitality with your family. It's a wonderful affirmation of your love.

~

*F*amily traditions are great, but there's nothing wrong with being flexible or allowing changes. Traditions can add joy and richness to life, but they don't have to go on forever. In our family, we used to reserve Friday evening for family nights. We'd eat popcorn, play games, whatever. As the children got older and their schedules changed, we moved our family time to Sunday. We'd all have breakfast together before church or go to brunch right after. Because we were willing to flex, our tradition of family time continued until our children got married. Traditions are meant to enhance our lives—not imprison us.

~

*B*irthdays are big deals in our family. Sometimes we throw a big blow-out party and other times it's a simple family affair. We always find special ways to make the person feel loved and appreciated. For instance, the birthday person always gets to pick out the dinner menu. We also commemorate anniversaries. In fact, we take advantage of every opportunity we have to honor someone. What are some good ways to have fun? Celebrate memories with a photo show or home videos. Extol your heritage with a special meal from the land of your ancestors and invite your friends. Throw a tea! (You knew I'd get *that* in somewhere, didn't you?) Organize a meet-your-neighbors party. And best of all, highlight what Ezekiel 34:26 calls "showers of blessings." Make a blessings list and then celebrate every one of them.

Your home is an expression of who you are. Whether you live in a small apartment, a condo, a large home in the suburbs, or a room in someone else's house, your place should reflect your special, personal taste. Fresh flowers don't cost very much, and they add a dash of color and sparkle to any room. Family photos, framed pictures from magazines, playful photos of baby animals can add zest to a room.

Let your imagination be your guide. If you're on a tight budget, think "spray paint." It works wonders on old frames, old furniture, and walls.

We all need a place where we belong, where we're comfortable. A place where we can unwind and regroup. Then we can truly share our lives with others.

~

*B*eing organized isn't the end-all of life. If you know me, you might think it odd that I would say that. I can't believe I said that either. If chaos and clutter in your home and life are wearing you down, the solution isn't a whirlwind effort to "get organized." You have to begin with your heart. God made us to worship Him and delight in Him. As we open our hearts to Him and put Him first, He will show us little ways to gradually address the chaos. Growing in the Holy Spirit is a lifelong, step-by-step process...and so is organization.

~

*L*ife is 5 percent joy, 5 percent grief, and 90 percent maintenance. In so many cases the most beautiful is also the most simple. A beat-up old table painted in a bright, happy color or a battered bucket with colorful flowers can bring a smile. Cost, size, and possessions have little to do with value. In fact, if we own too much we easily get to the point where we're merely "keepers of things." We can change our surroundings by using small touches. Put on your "creativity hat" and take a look around. Do you see what I mean? A little lace here, a basket or a candle there, and you've got the start of a new look...and outlook.

~

We teach best by what we are, not by what we say. I encourage you to be a "model woman" for your daughters and sons. Sarah Edwards, wife of famous preacher Jonathan Edwards, ran a household with no modern conveniences and reared many, many children. She sewed their clothes, cooked, gardened, made candles, and kept the home fires burning. She entertained hundreds of guests. She taught her children to work hard, to respect others, and to show good manners. Her life exemplified her values and her love for God. And it showed up in her children's accomplishments and attitudes. One of Sarah's grandsons became president of Yale University and said, "All that I am and all I'll ever be, I owe to my mother." The time you spend teaching your children can reach generations for Christ.

~

hey say you can tell by a woman's hairstyle the year she graduated from high school. I hope that isn't true. A few years ago I attended my 40-year high-school reunion. To put it nicely, the years were good to some and so-so to others. I was shocked to see how many of the popular kids in my class had experienced difficult times. I talked with others who were lesser known, and the opposite was true. This was a great reminder for me to not take myself too seriously.

Regardless of what others think of you, you're in God's hands. He cares for you no matter how well known or popular you were then or are now. First Peter 5:6-7 says God will "lift you up in due time. Cast all your anxiety on him because he cares for you." Isn't that wonderful!

~

have a confession to make. There are times when I feel totally ineffective in my life and in my prayer times. For instance, there was an awful time when I was extremely upset with my daughter for something she'd done. I prayed and prayed that there would be healing and a change of heart. Nothing changed. In fact, our relationship got worse. Can you identify with my anguished mother heart? The months passed. I complained to God, "Why haven't You answered my prayers?" The still small voice I heard said, "Ask your daughter for forgiveness." What! She was the problem—not me. But I finally went to her and apologized for my resentment and anger. When I did, the healing began. Such a simple idea, and yet so hard to implement. When we loosen chains of blame and resentment, God will work His miracles in our lives.

*N*eed a few simple tips for "breaking the ice"? What do you say when you meet someone new? What do you ask to get a conversation going? I've collected quite a few gems over the years.

- "Where did you live when you were six?"

- "What was your least favorite food as a child?"

- "Who was your first boyfriend (girlfriend)?"

- "What are the most encouraging words anyone can say to you?"

*W*ant a few ideas for reaching out to a single
friend? Many of my single friends tell me that
celebrating their birthdays can be the worst time of the
year. Even more difficult than Christmas sometimes.
So first, plan ahead...way ahead. My sources tell me
that the "what to do about my birthday" panic can
begin several months before the fateful day arrives.
Send your friend a pre-invitation card that says, "I plan
to celebrate your birthday with you!" Include a list of
dates you're available, and let your friend choose the
one that works best for her. Tickets to plays, a nice
dinner out, a spa outing for manicures or pedicures,
a day of shopping with lunch included are great ideas.
And the activity doesn't have to be expensive. Spending time together is the ultimate gift of friendship.

*A*dd a touch of hopefulness to your surroundings. For starters, take a cup of tea
into the room where you spend a lot of your time. (It
may even be your office.) Take the time to really look

at the colors, the arrangement of furniture, the decor. What about this room makes you feel energized and ready to move forward? Are there pictures of your family on your desk? Is light streaming in through the window? Do you have music playing in the background? Are flowers sitting on your table or desk? As simple as they sound, all these things can build a hopeful atmosphere. Nothing can bring the kind of hope that comes from trusting in God—He's the ultimate source. But creating a pleasant atmosphere certainly helps our moods and attitudes.

~

*R*emember way back in early school days when you planted a potato in a jar? Well, if you're a mom or a gramma, why not introduce fun traditions like that to the kiddos in your life? There's nothing like planting a garden to teach kids peacefulness, responsibility, and appreciation for God's creation. I love the idea of a "theme" garden for children. How about a pizza garden? You heard me—pizza! The kids can grow oregano, thyme, peppers, onions, and tomatoes. Make the entire experience creative and fun. Work together. And while you're at it, what great moments to share God's love and care. Ecclesiastes

12:1 says, "Remember your Creator in the days of your youth." And the garden is a great place to see His wondrous work.

~

*L*ittle details can make your home sparkle. Does that old countertop sink in your bathroom need a dash of style? Make a skirted vanity by attaching a curtain rod to the frame. Then hang white cotton fabric or a beautiful print picked up at a remnant sale. In minutes you've brightened the entire room. And thoughtful details will make your *life* glisten, as well. Spending time in God's Word, talking to Him, and listening to His still, small voice strengthens your relationship with Him. As the Bible reminds us in 2 Timothy 3:17, God is preparing and equipping you for every good work. Yep, it's all in the details!

~

*W*hen was the last time you told your daughter or your son what a treasure he or she is to you? Your words have a significant impact on your children. "You look so pretty today." "How smart you are." "What a killer smile!" "Your sense of humor is such a delight." Even though kids may not always say it, they hear you and revel in your positive encouragement. Psalm 127:3 grabs our attention: "Sons are a heritage from the LORD, children a reward from him." But it's not enough for you and me to know that truth. It's our responsibility as parents and grandparents to let the children in our lives know they are indeed treasures to our family. What a great gift!

~

I don't know about you, but I love to look at beautiful things. And sometimes those "things" are most unusual. Remember those old croquet balls we used to toss around the backyard when we were kids? Well imagine those colorful old (but cleaned up) balls in a beautiful wooden bowl on your dining room table. Or your grandmother's old clothespin bag filled with flowers on a kitchen wall. (Are you asking, "What is a clothespin bag?" Oh, I'm definitely revealing my age!) Keep an eye out for discarded items that can bring interest and flavor into your home.

~

*H*ave you ever thought you might be the answer to someone's prayer? I encourage you to visit a sick friend or call someone you know who needs a thoughtful word. Make this the day you write a check for the ministry that's been such a blessing in your life. Or surprise your sister with a bouquet of flowers. It might arrive at just the moment she needs encouragement. Before this sounds too much like a Hallmark card commercial, let me say that life is too short, relationships too precious, and God's messages too vital to not share them with friends and family. Hope isn't a feeling; it's something you do.

*W*hen I was little and behaved well, there was always a promise from my mom. I lived for comments like "Tomorrow we'll go to the beach" or "Be good and there will be ice cream for dessert." As a child, these promises were reasons to hope, to look forward to something nice. Because we're children of God, no matter what ages we are or what our life situations are, we have powerful reasons to hope because God has made us a lot of wonderful promises—and He always keeps His promises! He will be our strength, protect us, heal us, and never leave us. Why not read your Bible and discover more of His promises? How can we not be hopeful with all of His promises to experience and look forward to?

~

*I*s it old? And no, I'm not referring to me! The look for fall decorating is "old and comfortable." And that's the perfect time of year to bring out those afghans and the rich, warm-colored pillows you stashed away for the summer. One of the best inventions ever is "distressed" furniture. It's new—but it looks worn and comfortable.

Why not create a vanity corner in your bedroom? Set up an old table and chair, a mirror, some candles, a few flowers, a few decorative trays for makeup and odds and ends. Or an old tapestry footstool is a great place for a small stack of books. Look around. There are all kinds of ways to reuse what you have.

~

*L*et your house "tell a story" of the people who live there. And don't be afraid to have "mixed messages" in your decorating. Why not display a handful of seashells on an antique side table to remind you of that special vacation at the beach? The glitter of an old glass vase against a mirror or a traditional flower arrangement on a modern glass table creates beautiful contrast. You can fill your home with beautiful things, but true beauty is what's reflected in the lives of the people who live there. Psalm 149:4 reminds us that "the LORD takes delight in his people."

~

*Y*our home should be a place where you and your family members can relax and be yourselves. Sitting down together for a Thanksgiving dinner or a special birthday celebration is more about tradition than it is eating. Make these times special. Why not record them so you can remember and savor the events as the years pass by. Put extra effort into making special occasions memorable. Prayer times, family worship in front of the fireplace, listening to Grandma and Grandpa tell stories of their growing-up years create delightful lifelong memories.

~

*I*f you want a friendly and inviting home, why not paint or wallpaper? A few extra touches that

133

don't cost an arm and a leg can make your home shine. Paint the walls in colors you love. That sorry-looking old dresser becomes a decorator's dream with a coat of paint and some stenciling. And any room can be given a new touch of character with wallpaper. What a great invention!

~

*E*very bedroom needs a "nesting spot," a place where you and your child or grandchild can curl up and read a Bible story together. Find a comfy overstuffed chair big enough for two and establish a reading corner.

~

I encourage you to teach your children to pray. Prayer doesn't come naturally, not even for children. We have to build it into their lives. Pray with them often, and not just at mealtime or bedtime. I have a friend who prays out loud so her children are sure to hear her. And they're often surprised when she speaks their names. Encourage your kids to pray about their concerns and interests. If they're a bit older, why not start them journaling their prayers and thoughts? Boys and girls can create journals they'll love to go back and read when they get older.

~

*G*et out your pen and paper or laptop. Today we're making a list…a list of people to encourage this week. If you're having trouble thinking who that might be, let me give you a couple of ideas. Start with your family—even the ones you feel "iffy" about. Certainly your pastor and his family could use encouragement. The moms you know who are having a difficult time, neighbors, waiters and waitresses, the woman who works at the cleaners, the grocery store clerk who helps you often, people who've experienced recent loss—all could use pick-me-ups. First Thessalonians 5:11 says, "Encourage one another and build each other up." Get started today!

~

*Y*ou see it everywhere…and if I can do it, so can you. I'm talking about stenciling. As kids we did it on hard surfaces by outlining block letters using cardboard stencils. Now almost any surface is fair game, including curtains. And you can transform any glass surface, as long as you clean it with water and vinegar before you begin. Don't worry if it's not perfect—that's part of the charm. And the more expert you become, the more delightful the results. This reminds me of the imagery in Proverbs 3:3: "Let love and faithfulness never leave you...write them on the tablet of your heart"—and use stencils!

~

*C*ollecting has become a national mania. If you don't believe me, just check out *Antiques Roadshow,* one of the most popular shows on public television. Or you could come to my house. I can certainly prove that point by showing you my treasures. And then there's eBay. They say their mission is to help "practically anyone trade practically anything on earth!" Baskets, quilts, old toys, new toys, furniture, folk art, tools, baseball cards—our garages and homes and even storage units are filled to overflowing.

But do you know what's so interesting? *God's* emphasis for our lives is so uncomplicated. The Bible tells us, Sell what you have and give to the poor (Matthew 19:21). God will supply all your needs. With food and clothing be content. Are we supposed to dump all of our possessions? No, just keep them in the right perspective.

～

*B*utton, button, who's got the button?" This old rhyme reminds me that using something as ordinary as a button can make a great decoration. Why not put ribbon around a handmade card and use a glue gun to add a decorative button right in the middle of the card or at the top of the card? For a clever napkin ring, cover a piece of cardboard with fabric and tie with a ribbon. Decorate the fabric or the ribbon with buttons in colors that match your table setting. I'm sure you can come up with all kinds of ways to use colorful, unique buttons.

～

I saw a great headline the other day: "Never Have an Ordinary Day!" Now that's my kind of thinking. God gives you each day as a gift. Take a little time to make ordinary things extraordinary. A note to a friend doesn't have to be ho-hum. Add a pressed flower for her to enjoy. Get up a littler earlier and spend those moments getting ready for the day via a quiet time with the Lord. Make lunch or dinner an "occasion" at least once a week. You may be surprised at the reaction you'll get. Today is a gift, so take pleasure in unwrapping it.

~

*W*e all have family stories of times when God was faithful and merciful. Well, why not keep them for everyone to see and be reminded of on special occasions? Create what author Jeanne Zornes calls a "Faith Box." The one I saw included a hospital bracelet as a reminder of God's faithfulness in healing. There was a bag of broken glass symbolizing God's protection in an accident. In my box I'd have pictures of my children to remind me how faithful God has been to Bob and me in raising our family. And there would definitely be Scripture. What a wonderful way to record the faith moments in our lives.

~

I've learned that every day is good if I receive it with gratitude and enjoyment. Our days are gifts of grace given by a God who knows exactly what we need and when we need it. Don't spoil the joy by grousing that "good" days aren't "perfect" days. Why not do some "hope-giving" things today? Give thanks to God and the people you love. Deliberately store the moments of today in your memory. Share the day with someone you love. Write about the day in your journal or talk about it with your children. And when the day is over, let it go. Smile and sigh and trust God for tomorrow.

~

We should grab every opportunity to nurture our friendships. Get together with a friend even if it's to simply scrub each other's floors. Well, maybe not, but you know what I mean. Use your creativity to plan activities. Bake cookies or bread together. Deliver for Meals-on-Wheels one day a week. Organize a two-family garage sale and clean out both your attics and garages. Join together and take your kids on a field trip. Participate in a fun run for a favorite charity. And when you're all through with the project, share the satisfaction of a job well done and the joy of sharing it with a friend. "A friend loves at all times" (Proverbs 17:17).

~

Laughter is always the best medicine. And it's part of the fun of friendship. It literally feeds our joy. If you're a friend of mine, being silly once in a while is part of the plan. When you feel free to act absolutely goofy with a friend, you understand what the freedom of relationship is all about. Think about it. When was the last time you grabbed a friend and went to the park to swing? Or colored in a coloring book? When was the last time you giggled? Count yourself blessed if you have a friend who will be silly with you.

~

ake your home just a little more out of the ordinary. Rotating your pictures can give a whole new look to a room. Use "seasonal" frames if you can. A card table with matching chairs is one of the best investments you can make. Use it for patio or fireside dining or for additional guests at a dinner party. It can become a semi-permanent puzzle table. You'll be amazed at how fascinating a puzzle is to your guests. What matters is being able to sit and talk and play and share with your family and friends. Little touches can make a huge difference.

~

*T*ransferring values and traditions from one generation to the next is the joy of being a parent (and grandparent). And that's especially true with children. As we interact with our children and include them in our work and play, we're passing along family legacies. These are lessons best taught by the way we live. I love to hear Bob read Bible stories to our grandchildren. And I get a kick out of serving at a tea party for my granddaughter and grandsons. I'm passing along the value of manners and the joy of spending time together. Proverbs 22:6 requires that parents "train a child in the way he [or she] should go."

*B*ecoming a woman of God isn't always easy. First we have to make a personal commitment to Jesus. Second Corinthians 5:17 says, "If anyone is in Christ, he is a new creation; the old has gone, the new has come!" I was a 16-year-old Jewish girl when I received Christ. My life changed from that moment on. And believe me, it's been an adventure! God has guided me through pain and joy, struggle and growth. And sometimes I was kicking and screaming!

And God isn't finished with me yet. Far from it. I've discovered "becoming" is a lifelong process. And I have to be willing to change and learn what He wants to teach me. Are you willing to learn from Him?

~

I love it when my husband, Bob, and the children praise me. I also know times when I feel totally unappreciated. But God has taught me through those void periods to adjust my motivations and my expectations. When I stopped focusing on expecting people to react in a certain way, I began aiming to please God. When I quit expecting praise from my family, I started getting it. As women of God, we have the wonderful opportunity to let our lives sparkle with His love. And we'll become far less dependent on other people to make us feel worthwhile.

~

I talk to hundreds of women each year. Many of them are vainly trying to find the answers to two questions: "Who am I?" and "Why am I here?" Oh, they may not use those words, but pretty close. God has the answers for your life. I encourage you to set out on a journey to find satisfaction in them. Spend quality time in His Word. Talk to godly friends. Attend a biblically based church. And set aside part of each day to talk to God in prayer. He will show you the traits of the godly woman you've been created to be. Step out in obedience, depending on Jesus. It's an exciting pursuit.

~

*W*hy not "upgrade" your day? Instead of that quick cup of coffee, try a latte. Instead of choosing the same old trusty outfit, try a dash of bold color with a scarf or an unexpected piece of jewelry. Instead of sending an e-mail, write a note. Instead of sitting in the same seat you always do for church this Sunday, move to a different spot. You'll probably meet people you've never talked to before! Instead of watching TV, read a book. And instead of reading a bestseller, make it a classic. Make your life less ordinary. "This is the day the LORD has made; let us rejoice and be glad in it" (Psalm 118:24).

~

*D*ecorate your hotel room! Yep, you heard me correctly. Your hotel room. I don't know about you, but even when I travel I want to walk in and see something familiar and pretty. It could be something as simple as a bouquet of flowers purchased in the hotel flower shop. A friend of mine takes along a few family photos and sets them on the nightstand. (Just make sure they're copies of the originals in case something happens to them.) A candle, a little vase of dried flowers, pictures, your Bible and notebook— whatever you like. I guarantee it will make those days and hours away from home much more pleasurable.

～

*A*t the top of my remodeling list is making sure that anything I do complements how I live, including how I entertain and my needs for privacy, work areas, and room to play. It's good to think through all of these issues *before* you begin any project. The experts say, "Plan your space, and get it on paper." That means measuring and remeasuring. Any carpenter will tell you "measure twice, cut once." And come to think about it—that's a truism for life as well. The Bible says, "Give, and it will be given to you...For by your standard of measure it will be *measured* to you in return" (Luke 6:38).

～

*W*hen you're feeling discouraged, try your hand at writing a psalm. Before you start, read through some of the psalms in the Bible. Then follow that same pattern, and pour out your feelings to the Lord. Tell Him what's happening and how it makes you feel. Tell Him what you wish He would do. Then, as you write, let God bring you around to a statement of praise and trust. End the "song of your heart" on that note. Here's an example: "Lord, this is happening to me, and this is awful." Then tell Him exactly how you feel. A closing might be, "But You are my God, and You will work it all out. So I will praise You now."

*P*salm 19:7 says, "The law of the LORD is perfect, reviving the soul. The statutes of the LORD are trustworthy, making wise the simple." I spotted a decorating article recently with the title "Less Is Still More." The author said, "Simplicity is the highest form of sophistication." As soon as you get sidetracked by the "I wish I hads," your focus is turned away from what's really important. Mark 4:19 says, "The worries of this life, the deceitfulness of wealth and the desire for other things come in and choke the word, making it unfruitful." I encourage you to make the most of what you have.

~

I have a few helpful tips for you today. Try spraying just a bit of perfume on the light bulbs in your home. It creates a wonderful scent when the lights are turned on. Put a fabric softener liner in the drawers or closets with your towels or linens. Mmmm!

I love using candles, and I find they last a lot longer if I put them in the freezer at least three hours before burning them. If you've got a bunch of dusty artificial flowers ready to toss, clean them by putting some salt in a paper bag, adding the flowers, and shaking the bag. The salt absorbs the dust and dirt. Works like a charm!

~

*C*loth shopping bags are more chic than ever. I have them in all sizes, and I use them for holding everything. A friend of mine even used a little "black bag" as an extra evening tote for her camera. Even brown-paper bags make wonderful carryalls. Creatively use what you have.

~

A smart woman love, love, loves her husband. Yes, it takes years to learn patience, to bite your tongue, to overlook his faults. My Bob may not always be easy to love, but he's sure worth it. And who's the winner? I am! You can help make or break your home. The Bible says, "By wisdom a house is built, and through understanding it is established; through knowledge its rooms are filled with rare and beautiful treasures" (Proverbs 24:3). So let's not waste time arguing. Give God your family and you—failures and all. Commit to Him your attitude, your stress, and all the areas in which you need a sense of peace. Depend on Him to see you through the tough times. He will!

Have you noticed? It doesn't matter what you have, someone else always has something bigger or better. And what about those decorating magazines? Where do all those people find the time to decorate every nook and cranny of their homes? Maybe it's time to take a little break. Instead of focusing on "home beautiful," concentrate on what makes your home warm and caring. What makes it a place where you and your family can express your

God-given talents? No matter how little or how much you have, you can experience the results of a godly home. Make it a sanctuary, a place of security, trust, and comfort. That atmosphere can be set by you. There's no decorating scheme in the world that can replace the role you play in your home. It's that simple.

The closer it gets to wintry weather, the more cozy I like my house. One great idea is to place furniture so people can talk without having to shout across the room. Furniture against four walls isn't warm or cozy. If you've got a fireplace, create a seating area in front of it—a sofa facing two armchairs, with a coffee table in-between. Your home is communication central for your entire family. Cherish your moments with the people you love.

Here are some decorating tips...with a little extra tossed in for good measure!

- When you set out to decorate your home, give yourself time.

- Know what you *don't* want.

- Don't be afraid of color.

- Look for ways to save money.

- Show off your collections.

- Create a homey atmosphere with flowers, candles, and baskets.

And the little extra I promised? The most important tip is found in 2 Corinthians 9:8: "God is able to make all grace abound to you, so that in all things at all times, having all that you need, you will abound in every good work."

~

*N*eed a gift idea? How about a photo of you and your friend in a beautiful frame? Or a basket of items around a theme—tea, roses, the ocean, the mountains. A special dinner, tickets for a play, lovely candles work too. Select something with that person in mind—not just some old thing that's on sale or something you've had in the bottom of your dresser drawer. Good friends are few and far between. Cherish the ones you have.

~

*I*f your living room is small and you want to create an illusion of space, start by getting rid of the table lamps. Use wall sconces instead. And why have a three or four-seat couch? Do more than two sit on it very often? Keep your windows simple and unfussy. The walls should be painted in light colors to increase perception of space. And those items you love to have sitting around? Group them together, which makes them more interesting. *Living* room says it all. It's the "room" where we live, so make your living room a place where you and your family gather to enjoy each other's company.

*I*n life, going by the "we're climbing a mountain" analogy, the hope is we'll eventually get to the top, right? Well, that's where faith in God comes in. He's the One who enables us to keep our hopes up. As ho-hum as it may sound to you at this moment, I thrive on spending quiet time alone with God each day. It gives me perspective and hope. Those times are when I refresh by remembering my goals. And here's a tip for today: God knows the big picture for where you're going. In His Word He gives you and me what we need to make the journey successfully. This simple truth gives me hope.

~

*T*hank you for what you do for others. Have you considered the power of saying "thank you"? I overheard at a party recently the honoree jokingly saying, "Receiving all of these gifts means I'm going to have to write 'thank you' notes. Oh no!" He was kidding, but what got my attention, was someone else who quite seriously said, "Thank-you notes? I *never* send them." Whether you "write" notes or not, saying "thank you" is an important, nurturing expression. When you think about it, a major theme of Scripture is worship and praise. And that's another way of saying "thank you"!

~

*W*hat's a woman to do? Here are a few tips. First, be an excellent wife and mom—someone your husband and family can trust. Look out for their welfare. Be a woman who's here for them in every way, including providing good meals, working to help with expenses if necessary, and being a confidante. Do everything with strength, dignity, wisdom, and kindness. Keep yourself looking as good as possible, but make your emphasis the more important things.

What an incredible woman you are! And you thought being a Proverbs 31 woman was unattainable. The last verse of that inspiring proverb says: "Give her [that's you!] the reward she has earned, and let her hands bring her praise at the city gate." Indeed!

⁓

Is there something missing in the room's décor, but you're just not sure what it is? Decorating is all in the eye of the beholder, but here are some "try its" that might help when a room doesn't seem quite right.

- Change the lamp shades.

- Remove the books you've got stacked next to a chair.

- Change the curtains. That can spruce up just about any room.

- Remove some of the pillows—or change them.

- Rotate photographs once in a while.

Every Woman Should Know

- Change light bulbs for color or to be a softer light.

~

*P*roblem solvers—we all need them for the mundane stuff around the house and in our lives. For me a cup of tea, my prayer journal, and my Bible do the trick every time.

~

*N*eed some ideas for your next dinner party?

- Set the table in advance. It frees you up to "greet and chat," and your beautifully set table lets everyone know you're prepared.

- If you have several sets of china, why not "mix and match"? It makes each place setting look special and unique.

- Placecards are a great touch for seating people where you want them.

- It's always nice to have a little vase of flowers or maybe one of those tiny boxes of special chocolates for each guest to take home.

- Take pictures—one of each guest with you.

153

You can send the photos to the people later…
as another special touch to show you care.

~

*E*ncourage your family members by meeting
together and studying God's Word. You don't
have to take up an entire evening if your schedules are
tight, but make it a part of your regular family happenings. Pray for one another, read out of the Bible,
share what God's been teaching. The most influential
Christian instruction your child gets will come from
you. Proverbs 22:6 says to "train a child in the way
he should go." And you will benefit tremendously as
you learn more and see God at work in each person's
life.

~

*W*hy do we pray? The obvious answer is "to
communicate with God." But I want to suggest something beyond that. Today, why not take the
time to pray for someone else? When you do, it'll
tone down that "me" attitude we're all guilty of. It'll
help you focus on someone else—your son, daughter,
spouse, good friend, pastor, coworker. What does
each person need? And there's a side benefit for you

too. As you pray, you'll draw closer to God, and this helps you find out what He wants. Take the time today to be the woman God wants you to be!

~

*M*arriage is a lot of work. There. I said it. Wimps need not apply! I hope these few "words of wisdom" will be an encouragement.

- A good marriage isn't a gift; it's an achievement by God's grace.

- Marriage isn't for children; it takes guts and maturity. It definitely separates the women from the girls.

- Marriage is giving, and more importantly, *forgiving*.

- Scripture gives us hope by promising us that if we give proper honor to marriage, we will be honored by our children, our families, our neighbors, our friends...and best of all, by our Lord.

~

*W*ant some creative ideas for Thanksgiving decorations? You can count on me!

Pumpkins are wonderful right up until the end of the month. Their color and size make a statement like nothing else. Place a medium-sized pumpkin on a pedestal cake platter for the center of your table. Decorate it with vines and a few clusters of berries. On a table runner, arrange candles, pinecones, and mini gourds. Sprinkle fall-colored glitter, and you're all set for the holiday.

~

*I*f you're looking for something to do on a crisp, cool Saturday morning, how about a walk in the park? C'mon! When was the last time you did that? And if it were me, I'd grab a grandchild to take with me. And I wouldn't be Emilie Barnes if there wasn't a practical angle in this. While you're enjoying the wonderful time together, bring back items you can use later to decorate for the holidays: pinecones, twigs, leaves, vines. They make beautiful centerpiece items or for setting around as natural art. And what fun to do this with a child or grandchild!

~

*H*ave you known someone with limited income who's rich? A friend of mine takes great delight in going to second-time-around stores and purchasing very nice clothing at greatly reduced prices. Another friend takes old furniture and gives it her artistic touches. Another couple loves to camp along the California coastline. For very little cost they visit a different state every year and have a great time with their family. You can find happiness within a budget. Instead of spending time thinking about what you don't have, count your blessings for what you do have.

*O*n those days when you'd just as soon crawl back into bed rather than face all that you have to do, put your feet on the floor and take that first step of the day. When I'm able to break a large day into small pieces, it's not nearly as overwhelming. And you know what? I usually manage to get everything done—and sometimes I even laugh along the way. Tomorrow when you wake up, what's the first thing you need to do? Do it! What's the second thing? Do it too. Go one step at a time and thank God for each new beginning.

*I*nvolve your children in prayer times with you. Let them give you some prayer requests and you share some of yours. Bob and I started doing this when our children were in high school. Breakfast was the only meal when we were together as a family, so that became our sharing time. We'd ask, "What kind of exam are you going to have today?" Or they might ask me about a speaking engagement. Afterward, when we were together again, we'd have a point of reference: "How did your exam go?" This is a great way to make prayer a part of your life as a family. Jesus said, "Where two or three come together in my name, there am I with them" (Matthew 18:20).

~

*W*ant to maintain your sanity during holidays? Plan, plan, plan! Start now to schedule some of the activities so your load will be lighter later on. Even if you've never done it before, start being a woman with a to-do list in hand. Jot down groceries you're going to need, gifts to buy, cards to purchase—put everything on one big list. Then parcel them out throughout the weeks and put them on your calendar so you know exactly what to do each week between now and the holidays.

~

*I*n 1843 Henry Cole decided to write all of his friends at Christmastime. And his idea has led to mass-marketing holiday cards. If you're going to send cards, make them meaningful. Always add a handwritten note on the standard greeting that's engraved. I love to include and receive family pictures. And the annual holiday letters? Well, if they bring me up-to-date on people I care about, I enjoy reading them and praying for the people mentioned. Keep your holidays simple and sincere.

~

*T*hanksgiving dinner is such a wonderful occasion to see family and celebrate the season. The table and centerpiece are the big decorations for the event. Use material you have on hand—dried flowers, candles, teacups, even family photos lined up along a lovely table runner. Wouldn't it be fun to feature old pictures of everyone attending your Thanksgiving dinner?

~

*G*od knows the desires of your heart. That's pretty astounding, isn't it? And He wants you to ask Him for those desires. Just be sure to check yourself by saying, "Lord, if it wouldn't be good for me to have this, then I really don't want it. But if it would be okay with You, I'll be very grateful and use it for Your glory." Then be prepared! God always answers. It may be an immediate yes, a "wait a while," or a no. Allow God to work in your life with His love. He will always give you what is best. And remember to thank Him in *all* things.

*I*f you love baking, put on some great praise music, get all your ingredients out, and make it a party. It's a wonderful occasion to involve your grandchildren. And here's a baking gem from my mama: If you cover dried fruits or nuts with flour before adding them to the batter, they won't sink to the bottom during baking.

A friend of mine told me her family always drew names for Christmas gift-giving for the adults during their Thanksgiving holiday.

Everyone would put their name on a slip of paper that was then put in a bowl. The names were drawn by the youngest of the little ones. They made quite a ceremony out of it. And the result was not only a lot of fun at their Thanksgiving dinner, but something to look forward to on Christmas Eve. They also set a reasonable price limit, so everyone could stay within their budgets.

I love giving gifts to everyone! That being the case, I have to start early. November is always the time I ask my family to make wish lists for Christmas. And then I have all sorts of ideas as I do my shopping. There's none of that guesswork that is so time consuming and frustrating. Keep your sense of humor and perspective during the holidays. Keep the season wide open for warmth, fellowship, shared experiences, lots of hospitality, and celebrating the true reason for Christmas—Jesus.

I don't have a messy house, but it is full! Why do I have so many things? Some of them just kind of happened my way. But so many of our precious belongings were given to me by people I love. Tablecloths, linen, lace, and teacups galore. And I admit they're tangible expressions of who Emilie Barnes *looks* like. But despite my attachment for many of these items, they are not my life. They are "my stuff." When we're thankful for the love we have around us, the possessions we have will be in proper perspective. The next time you sit down with your family, thank God for all He's given you.

~

*A*re you traveling with children? Be prepared with plenty of things to do. Take small toys, games, and snacks and wrap them like presents. Every hour of the trip, give each child a gift to open. It's amazing the difference gift-wrapping and presents make in their attitudes. By the time they get tired of one thing, it's time to open another one.

~

*W*hen traveling with kids, use one large bag can hold an entire outfit for a child. Use a bag for each day, and you won't leave anything behind.

~

There's a lot of comfort in maturity. I know this from experience! Yes, some people believe that "mature" is just another word for admitting we're old. But think about it a moment. The word really means "seasoned" and "beautiful." Hmmm…I'm sensing I haven't convinced you. Think of it this way. You've learned how to touch, how to give, and how to keep your mouth shut when it's appropriate. And you know when to speak up. And isn't it great that some things are no longer important, such as status and always being right? And yet other things, like keeping promises and being trustworthy, have become priorities. Hebrews 6:1 reminds us to "leave the elementary teachings about Christ and go on to maturity [in Him]." Maturity is one of life's most astonishing gifts.

"Conduct is what we do; *character* is what we are." The world waits until someone gives before giving back, but Scripture tells us to give first, and then it will be added to us. A note of encouragement, a phone call, a surprise dinner invitation, a special treat to commemorate a job well done, a love basket, a promise to pray…the list is endless of ways you can bless someone. When we give to others, God is pleased. If you're waiting for someone to give to you before you're willing to give to her, try the reverse. You give first. That gesture may make all the difference in your relationship.

hy have a meal, I say, when with a little planning it can be a celebration! Make the next Thanksgiving holiday special. You don't have to spend a lot of money, just put more thought into what you can do. Focus on sharing and appreciation activities. Get out the candles, the beautiful fall leaves, gourds, pumpkins, and flowers for Thanksgiving. Prepare the turkey and all the goodies just the way you like it. Then sit down, clasp your hands together in blessing, and rejoice in your family, friends, and the food God has provided.

reate wonderful memories. One holiday idea is a cookie exchange. It's a stroke of genius, actually. You make a batch of cookies and swap them for a lot of other different kinds. Have a party and invite your friends to bring several dozen made from their favorite recipes. It's fun and you're all set for the rest of the season. Family videos during the holidays are wonderful memory-makers. Or why not write your Christmas cards as a family? And best of all, think of others. Sign up to help feed the homeless. Give toys, adopt a family for the holidays, or take special treats to some shut-ins you know. And don't forget the various charities that assist people in need. As you're thankful for what God has given you, pass it on.

~

One of the great joys in life is to give thanks to God. It's important to gather our families and friends together for prayer at special times, including celebrations and times of transition. A simple grace at mealtime is a tradition that honors the God of all gifts. Offering thanks doesn't make the food into something it isn't, but it does make those who eat the food more appreciative. Teaching our children the language of gratitude is a gift to them. Psalm 69:30 says, "I will praise God's name in song and glorify him with thanksgiving."

~

Christmas is coming! And here are a few hints and tips to keep the holiday more relaxed.

- Remember what really matters—Jesus, family, friends.

- Hassles will often take care of themselves.

- It's okay to say no.

- You can't be everywhere and see everything.

- Don't be afraid to back off.

- Plan some time for yourself to relax or read a book.

- Listen to some soothing music while you do other things.

- Buy a new Christmas robe.

In other words, take care of yourself, Mom! Celebrating God's gift of His Son, family, and friends—that's the true meaning of the season.

~

"This is the day the LORD has made, let us rejoice and be glad in it!" I can't think of a better way to start the day. When you begin in a "frenzied flurry," that's pretty much the way it'll go all day. I've been there, done that. Instead, make your mornings *hope full*. Put on your favorite snuggly bathrobe, enjoy a quiet cup of coffee or tea, maybe have a little music playing in the background. Open your Bible to a favorite passage, read a bit, and then ask God for the strength and courage to spend the day in hope. Give the day clarity and meaning. Hold every moment sacred.

~

*B*ad days are a given. You might as well expect 'em and plan for them.

- Remember that 24 hours from now this day will be over.

- Fill your heart with Scripture and prayer, *especially* if you don't feel like it.

- Go ahead and gripe—a little bit.

- Count to ten before you respond to anyone.

- Pay a little more attention to yourself when you're having a bad day.

- I know it doesn't seem possible, but some bad days come with hidden blessings—a word of encouragement, a life lesson that finally clicks, a confirmation that some things need to change.

Hope grows in a variety of circumstances, including rotten days.

*T*ake a chance—you may be surprised at what happens. Here's how it works. Instead of wishing you were thinner, how about taking a walk? Instead of wishing for a friend, ask someone to lunch. Instead of wishing you could help, sign up to drive for Meals-on-Wheels or help in an outreach at your church. Oh, you could pull a muscle walking or that person you invite for lunch could turn you down, but the more you hole up inside in a safe little place the more you lose out on wonderful possibilities. And others miss out on knowing you. Go ahead—make today the day you step out and try something new.

*M*akeovers are always fun, but what about a "makeover" for your day? Why not color outside the lines? Almost any daily routine can be made more fun by being just a bit different. Consider a change in menu. Serve breakfast for dinner! How about setting up a tent indoors for your kids to play in? They'll love the surprise and novelty. Set up a candlelight dinner for your husband and arrange for a babysitter for the kids. Hold a picnic in the living room. The idea is to not let a day pass exactly like the day before. Create and experience "moments"! One wise person said, "It's amazing how much planning goes into being spontaneous."

~

*D*ressed up or dressed down, color can make all the difference. My mother always said, "Once you've got the basics, just add color. If the gold tones in your chair appeal to you, why not paint the ceiling the same color? If you love beautiful wood tones, let it serve as the palette for the colors you add.

When we lift someone else's load we add color to our lives. Why not visit the sick, mow a neighbor's lawn, encourage a coworker, volunteer at a local shelter, or teach a Sunday school class?

~

*U*se ornaments as gift. Look for special ornaments that fit your friends' personalities. Then, when you're visiting friends or going to holiday parties, you have the perfect hostess gifts to leave behind. Write the year on the back to make it a keepsake. Be creative! There's no end to what can be made into a gift.

~

*C*hristmas is one of my favorite times of year—a time for friends, for giving, for eating wonderfully prepared goodies, for hearing favorite Christmas carols, for decorating our home in reds and greens. Before you think I'm the perfect "Miss Christmas," you need to know I do a lot of planning to make sure I enjoy as much of the holiday as possible. By planning when I need to decorate, bake, and wrap those last-minute gifts, I enjoy the season so much more. But all the planning, the decorating, the wonderful food is meaningless if I don't take the time to remember that Jesus is the best gift of all!

~

*I*nstead of tossing out Christmas cards, birthday cards, and any other card you receive, keep them in your prayer basket. Use them to pray for the people who sent them to you.

~

I can't think of anyone who doesn't like the special touch of a homemade gift. Okay—maybe I can think of some—but the point is still a good one. It's amazing what a basket of specially baked goodies can mean to a friend, a neighbor, or a teacher. I guarantee it will be a hit. Add some colorful tissue and a beautiful ribbon to jazz up your sweet gift. Be sure to personalize your gift by the choice of baskets, jars, and containers.

N eed a special Christmas gift? Think outside your usual box. For a hostess gift, a miniature pine with a small sparkling ornament or perhaps an elegant amaryllis will complement any Christmas decor. Gifts that encourage "stay-at-home" time, such as a board game or a classic movie on DVD work well too. Package it in a beautiful basket with popcorn. For children, stuffed toys, a tea party set, dollhouse, train sets, ranch sets, farm trucks please little hearts. Make this a time of giving from a heart filled with gratitude for the gift *you've* been given—Jesus Christ.

*I*f you've waited until the last minute to do your shopping, here are a few simple ideas that work for me.

Now's the time to put all those baskets you've been saving to good use. Filled with wonderful gift items, they are the perfect answer to last-minute shopping. Fill one with soaps, bubble bath, special candles and your basket is ready for giving. Or how about favorite magazines, a few books, a bookmark, and a high-intensity light for the bookworm on your list? You can have lots of fun with your basket themes. Wrap them with cellophane or tissue and a beautiful ribbon.

*K*eep the holiday season hassle free!

- It's okay to say no. You'd like to do it all, but sometimes you need to set limits. Say, "We need this time together as a family" or "No, I can't bake the extra cookies, but I'd be happy to buy some."

- Plan time for yourself.

- Watch your finances carefully. Overspending definitely creates tension and depression.

Celebrating family, friends, and the true meaning of Christmas is what counts.

~

*C*andles are beautiful and practical!

- Help your candles burn brightly by storing them in the freezer until you're ready to use them. This keeps them from dripping or sparking when they're lit.

- To make sure they stand properly and firmly, add a little florist's clay in the base of the candleholder.

- If this is one of those years when your decorating dollars are stretched to the max, think candles. They bring a beautiful light to any setting, to say nothing of all the things that stay hidden in the shadows.

~

*T*here's nothing better than the smell of cookies when you walk in the door. And make mine chocolate chip! Cookies make a great gift, and creating them with your children or grandchildren is a wonderful tradition to start. You'll grow closer and they get some good experience in the kitchen.

Put your cookies on colorful paper plates or mismatched china plates you've bought on sale. Add a bit of cellophane and a bow, tuck in a little note, and you have a sweet gift!

And what a great way to involve children as you deliver your special plates of cookies to elderly neighbors, friends, and acquaintances. Teach your children the art of creative giving.

~

Whether married or single, you can create lasting traditions. Start the year by creating a photo book filled with photographs you took the previous year. Make it a fun project by including creative and funny captions and the background stories. Label all the people so you'll know who they are in the many years to come.

~

Whether you're filling Christmas stockings or putting together little "thinking of you" gifts, here are some fun tips for adults and children:

- Small, stuffed teddy bears
- colored pens or pencils
- little puzzles and games
- a magazine subscription
- socks
- belts
- hair clips
- CDs
- shampoos, lotions, and body washes
- kitchen items
- theater tickets
- golf balls

Be creative coming up with the things that will be fun for your family and friends.

Why not set aside a day this month to sort through your memories, pray for discernment to understand how God brought you to where you are today, and look back on your life with thanksgiving? In gratitude for God's presence, open your eyes to what He is doing today and what He might have for you in the future. If your heart is tuned to see God working today, you'll be more likely to look forward to tomorrow—and be encouraged!

*W*hy not plan a special ceremony to pass along a family heirloom to a child or friend? Or why not make one day this week special by doing something out of the ordinary for someone?

*I*f you're feeling a little shook up over the circumstances of your life, don't despair. Remind yourself that the process may well be God getting you ready for something new and wonderful. Don't fight what's going on. Instead, listen, be still, seek the Lord diligently in prayer, and read His Word expectantly. Envision yourself stripped for action—sleek, beautiful, ready to do His will. Some things have to die in order for new life—and new hope—to begin. With God, death is never the last word.

*I*f you want to make your house a home but have a tight budget, I can help.

- Number one is to paint the walls a favorite color.

- Proudly display your collections. (My teacups are in special groupings all around my home.)

- Frame those favorite photographs. Put some of them in your bathroom.

Isn't this sounding easier all the time?

- Creatively use plants and flowers. Change them to match the seasons.

- Fill each room with heavenly scented candles.

It doesn't take much to make a change in the way your home looks and feels.

~

*F*or a creative touch in your bedroom, clean up a weathered old door from a flea market and add some legs. With a few personal items arranged on the top of your "new" table—you've got a country look going. A fresh coat of paint does wonders for any room. Paint just one wall. It'll make a statement without overpowering the whole room. Your home, regardless of how much or how little money you spend, is an expression of you.

~

*N*eed to get in the right "frame of mind"? If you have a collection of frames with nothing to fill them, think again! With a mat board you can create a wonderful organizer frame for your kitchen wall. Add seamstress tape to the top edge of each strip to create "pockets." Or paint your frames a single color and hang them as a group on a colored wall. It becomes a graphic, even if you decide not to put any pictures in the frames. And what child's room can do without a cork board for all their special "stuff." Just frame it and hang it.

~

*W*hen you're passionate, your enthusiasm is contagious! When you get involved in an activity or a project that you really love to do, you suddenly get out of yourself. You may be volunteering with at-risk children, helping the elderly, coaching a sports team, teaching knitting, or creating memory books—whatever you're excited about doing is worthwhile. One author said, "Every hobby teaches you something." What are you learning?

~

*R*emember when you were a child and well-meaning adults would say, "Now, don't get your hopes up." They meant well. Their intent was to protect you from disappointment, from having your hopes crushed. Today you may have prayed for a raise, or a new home, or even a spouse. You waited. You trusted. And it didn't happen. And it hurts. So should you give up hoping? No! What you need to do is strengthen your trust in your heavenly Father and His love. Keep your hopes high knowing God will help you handle the disappointments, and He only wants to give you the things that will be good. When you're tempted to say, "This is hopeless," try saying instead, "I wonder what God's going to do next?"

~

*N*eed to travel light?

- Emilie's first rule of travel is "Don't take more luggage to the airport than you can carry yourself." If you can't carry it, you're taking too much.

- Clean out your purse or tote bag before you leave. There's at least a pound of stuff in there you don't need for a trip, including ticket stubs, loose change, and receipts.

- Have an expandable tote bag so you can carry all the souvenirs and gifts you plan to buy.

- For practice, pack normally...and then take out half the clothes. Yep—half! And all those shoes? I don't think so!

Traveling light is a concept for *every* area of life.

A vacation in Hawaii? Someone to clean your house? A spa day? None of those may seem possible right now, but here are some easy ways to give your spirits a lift:

- Pick up a few gorgeous flowers at the florist and enjoy them.

- Use your special china every day.

- If you work outside the home, once a week go out for lunch to the nicest place you can afford.

- Indulge in a small luxury, such as a special coffee or tea.

- Allow yourself some quiet time in the Word with the Lord. That makes everything better.

~

A wonderful Christmas tradition is caroling. I love spreading the special sounds of Christmas to friends and neighbors. "Jingle Bells" and "White Christmas" are fun to sing, but also include songs that praise God. Include a shelter or a rest home on your list of places to sing. Music spreads joy to those who may not be celebrating with family and friends.

~

*G*od has gifted you in ways you may not even be aware of. My husband, Bob, and I were well into our adult years before we became writers. Who knew that would happen? God has used our ability to connect with people to encourage and motivate millions of women and men. And it literally changed our lives. If you want to discover your gifts, you'll need to do some experimenting. But it's more than worth the risk. Perhaps your hidden talent is teaching, writing, artistic ability, or innovative thinking. I guarantee that once you start trying out different areas of service, you'll discover dozens of hidden gifts—even if you're in your seventies or eighties.

*I*f you're feeling guilty about all that needs to be done around the house, let the negative feeling go. There's always going to be some kind of mess to clean up.

*I*f you're spending more time in your kitchen but *enjoying* it less, it's time for a few changes.

- If space is part of the problem, store pots on a hanging rack.

- Put "like items" together, such as spices and oils.

- Use baskets to keep things organized.

- Spruce up your kitchen window with some glass shelves and plants.

- You can brighten any kitchen by painting the ceiling white.

- Why not install wonderful under-cabinet task lights? What a difference they can make. Or perhaps add a lamp for soft lighting.

*W*hat to do with all those leftovers? And the leftovers I'm talking about today are *household* leftovers.

- Use wallpaper pieces for gift wrap and for covers for scrapbooks or boxes.

- Leftover paint is great for shelves, baskets, and touch-ups.

- Cards are wonderful to use as artwork inside frames.

- I heard of a woman who took an old suitcase,

183

cut off the top, and lined it. Then she had a perfect dog bed.

- Even beads from an old necklace make great decorating touches for a lamp shade or the edge of a picture frame.

Check out your leftovers and put them to good use.

~

*I*f you're feeling unloved, you're not alone. God doesn't stop loving us, but like naughty, confused children, we often pull away from His loving arms. What can you do to cheer yourself up?

- Underline the verses in your Bible that remind you how much you're loved by God. For instance, God said, "I have summoned you by name; you are mine" (Isaiah 43:1). Read those verses over and over.

- Hang around with loving, giving people. Those attributes are contagious.

- Practice delight. The more you notice and delight in what God has created, the better you'll be.

- Show love to others. Your acts of thoughtfulness and kindness will rub off—on you.

*I*f you've got that cluttered or claustrophobic feeling, you've come to the right place. Here's a great guideline: For every purchase you bring into the house, something else has to go. With a new blouse or shirt, out goes an older one. A new table? Out goes the former one. These items are great for a garage sale. Life can get very complicated, and stuff seems to accumulate. Then that "bunched in" feeling occurs. So the next time you purchase an item, give a like item away or set it aside for a garage sale. Become a giver!

*T*oday I encourage you to do what you say you're going to do. We get into trouble when we don't keep our promises. And sometimes we're not even aware we've made a promise. We say, "I'll call you tonight" or "I'll get back to you to set a date for lunch," but don't follow through. Does this sound familiar? Get out of the habit of offering to do things you might not do. Your friends would rather not hear an "I will do" statement if it's not going to happen. A friend of mine says, "It takes so little to be above average." And she's right! Develop a reputation for being a woman who does what she says. Your life will have more meaning and people will enjoy being around you.

〜

little "thank you" goes a long way. Never take anything for granted. When you do something courteous for your husband, use it as an opportunity to remind him that he's loved. Say, "This is just another way to show that I love you." This may sound terribly old-fashioned, but be willing to treat that guy of yours like a king...so he will treat *you* like a queen.

〜

love garage sales and flea markets. You just have to know what to look for and how to use it. If you're fortunate enough to find an old milking stool, grab it. A little paint and you have a new little table. Find old-fashioned paper dolls? Arrange them in a frame for a young girl's room. The key to decorating with—do I dare say it—old junk is looking at it with a new eye. A marble-topped dresser can be a beautiful dining room cabinet. Gilded frames? Put them in the kitchen. With simple creativity, your home has new sparkle. And no one will ever know it used to be junk.

~

I had a very close friend who often said things like, "If only I could have a bigger house...a bigger car...a bigger ring—then I'd be happy." And you know what? Twenty-five years later she's still looking for happiness. The Bible says that a thankful heart is a happy heart. When I'm grateful for all I have, life seems to be in balance. My work goes smoother, and the mood in our home is more relaxed. The truth is, people like to be around people who are positive and encouraging, who build up instead of tear down. Take time today to give thanks for all that God has given you and your family!

~

*I*f your husband no longer opens the car door for you, maybe it's time to make changes. And no, I'm not talking about getting a new husband. Did you know that "taking a mate for granted" is one of the main reasons there is a 50 percent divorce rate? Don't get caught in that trap. Step back and make sure you're filling each other's emotional tanks. Appreciation is a choice, so choose to be grateful and express your love. The more you do, the easier it becomes.

~

here's an old story about a clock that began to think how many times during the year ahead it would have to tick: 31 million, 536 thousand seconds in one year. The clock was exhausted at just the thought and said, "I can't do it." But when the clock was reminded it didn't have to tick the seconds all at one time—only one by one—it began to run again and everything was hunky-dory. When we break our days into small pieces they become much more manageable too. We can even laugh along the way because we're not so stressed. A long journey begins with the first step.

~

ometimes the best idea for decorating is taking a second look. One woman said, "My collections on display inject a dash of color and originality into my home." How right she is. Sometimes an "old treasure" just needs a new container. Buttons in jars or a flowered hat under a glass cake dome create interest. Old suitcases stacked in a corner create a wonderful new conversation piece, especially if they have a travel sticker or two attached. If one thing looks good, multiples look even better. Jewelry on a pegboard and purses and hats on a wall in your bedroom are fun. Let your imagination have a heyday!

*L*et me share a few simple thoughts from my heart to yours. I definitely believe in taking care of myself and my surroundings. But if I put all my energy into just taking care of my outward self, I miss the real point of life. True beauty begins *inside*. And if it's lacking there, no exercise program, eating plan, or wardrobe can fix it. Ruffles and perfume are no substitute for God-given beauty. I need the message of 1 Peter 3:3-4: "Your beauty should not come from outward adornment…Instead, it should be that of your inner self, the unfading beauty of a gentle and quiet spirit, which is of great worth in God's sight." This is interior decorating *God's* way!

I love all the artwork children do at school, Sunday school, or at home. I remember reading that TV star Carol Burnett beautifully framed all her children's artwork. She hung them on a wall in her home for all to see. If you have a bit more than you can hang, why not use some of it for wrapping paper? Or have your child select their favorites and put them in a scrapbook to enjoy and pass along to their own children. Mount them on cardboard or lovely fabric, and you get the perfect placemats for their next birthday party or a family party. What a perfect way to affirm a child's creativity.

L eave a legacy that will impact generations of women! We teach best by who we are, not by what we say. Teaching our daughters to be lovely is so much more than cooking and cleaning. It's teaching values and caring for ourselves spiritually and physically so that we can care for others. The joys and responsibilities—and yes, even the pain and the challenges of womanhood—that we pass along to our daughters will benefit generations of wives and mothers and singles to come.

*I*t's not always easy to carve out time for developing friendships, but in my opinion it's not an option. Friends share the load of living. Every Saturday morning, Evelyn and her best friend, Sharon, meet by phone—Evelyn from California and Sharon from Michigan. They've been doing their Saturday morning "friend" calls for 25 years. I suggest you block out times together with your good friends to play, to talk, to shop. My dear friend Donna and I consider our times together an absolute necessity to healthy, happy living. Although we live in different states, each year we block out special times to spend together. It's a priority for us. We even wrote a book together. Now that's a true test of friendship!

I love those TV programs where they take old treasures and turn them into something beautiful and useful. It could be an old stamp collection or an old set of dishes. Have you noticed what collectors are paying for old autographs? No matter what you have, it can be revitalized and used in decorating your home. The best place to put these treasures is out in the open. Stack old books and Bibles on shelves and have lamps and tables nearby where they can be read and enjoyed. Cluster a group of pictures on a table. Spread quilts on your beds. Make your home a reflection of love and warmth, of giving and caring.

~

*L*ooking for wonderful decorating treasures? Go to garage sales. Be one of the first to arrive. It's not only fun to look, but keep your eyes open for that item you've always wanted. Keep a list with you of what will complement your current decorating—or will even make a good gift. In today's throw-away society, these treasure hunts are refreshing and the perfect way to spend sunny days. Okay, *any* day!

~

*W*hy not plan menus two weeks at a time and shop for everything at once? It's a real time-saver.

~

*P*icture frames are one of today's hottest decorating items. They come in all shapes, sizes, and styles: glittery, glass, wood…anything you can imagine. What do you put in all those lovely frames? I'm so glad you asked! How about old postcards, along with pictures of you and your family at Yosemite or on another vacation trip? Children's artwork, hats, and seashells you picked off the beach last summer look great framed. Illustrated tiles, music, even some music instruments…just hang them on the wall and add a frame around them. Let your creativity and sense of fun flow freely.

~

hy not give a favorite recipe as a gift? One of my best is a triple-chocolate cake recipe. Everyone loves it, and it's so easy. It only takes three steps and five minutes. I give a decorative copy of the recipe, a package of chocolate chips, a box of chocolate pudding, and a box of chocolate cake mix.

~

f you're a member of the "I Can't Club," make a change. Yes, the "I Can't Club" is very popular and has members all over the world. Under the by-laws, members are required to make "I can't" statements with conviction. "I can't help hating him after what he did." "I can't quit drinking…or smoking…or stealing…or being unfaithful." "I can't forgive." When you accepted Christ as your Savior, God opened the pathway for you to access His strength. Romans 8:2 says, "The law of the Spirit of life set me free from the law of sin and death." When God fills your spirit with His Spirit, you are no longer captive to any temptation. The choice is yours. Change your "I can't" to "I *can*!"

~

What are you sharing with your daughter to bring special value to her life? One woman I know makes a practice of sharing a "note book" with her eight-year-old daughter. They take turns writing messages and leaving it for the other to find. It may show up on the daughter's bed with a note of encouragement or a special Bible verse after school. Then it'll find its way, along with an answer, to the mother's desk. The whole idea was to create a way of communicating with her daughter during times when talking may be difficult. And what a wonderful keepsake these exchanged notes will become. Handwritten and personal encouragements engrave "You are loved" on our hearts.

~

*W*e need to get in the habit of under-promising and over-delivering. When someone asks you to pray for them, do you do it? I confess I sometimes forget. I don't mean to, but the busyness of life takes over and the promise to pray is often forgotten. Finally I started a prayer notebook that I carry to church with me. It's an inexpensive notepad that I added a "prayer request" tab to. When people come up and ask me for prayer, I either pray with them on the spot or note their requests in my notebook to remind me later to pray. This works like a charm! Why not try it? You'll be surprised how much more exciting life becomes as you see God working through your prayer requests. And best of all, you'll begin to see the sovereignty of God as you pray. Jot down those prayer requests. It's part of the blessing of a well-ordered life.

*W*ork doesn't need to be a drag. I'm afraid we're losing a lot of our enthusiasm for the blessing of work. That's right, it should be a blessing. We'd be a lot happier if we recaptured the idea that our work, our wealth, and our possessions are all gifts from God. As children of God, we should be the best and most enthusiastic workers of all. The Bible says, "Whatever you do, work at it with all your heart, as working for the Lord" (Colossians 3:23).

~

I'm ready for tea! Will you join me?" When you're planning a party, remember to keep it simple. Plan it for a time of the year when you can use flowers from your own garden. Bring out your dishes, even if they aren't fine china. Make your table setting as beautiful as you can. Serve a variety of teas, along with some cinnamon sticks for flavoring, if you have them. Scones and heavy cream are standard tea fare. Soft music in the background gives a wonderful setting for your friends to enjoy. As you enjoy tea together, give each of your guests a little card that says, "Thank you for your loving friendship." Have every guest share the blessings she or he's experienced recently.

~

*E*veryone needs a place she can call her own. For me, it's the bedroom. It isn't always my own, of course, but you know what I mean. It's my dressing room, my reading room, my private retreat when

I need one. Where's your room? Make it comfortable and appealing. If you like the look of fabric, go with a canopy look over the bed. Create an interesting headboard. And just about any small piece of furniture will work as a nightstand. Drape a cloth of soft shades of color over a round table. Keep the lighting soft and soothing. Make your room a place where you can read your Bible, pray, and write in a journal undisturbed. Enjoy *your* special place.

~

our quiet time with the Lord isn't a gift you give Him—it's His gift to you. Make it a habit to say, "Good morning, Lord" and "Good evening, Lord." Start and end the day by acknowledging Him. You'll be surprised at what this does for your day and night. And it's a wonderful alternative to only asking for wants and concerns. Be thankful for the prayers your heavenly Father has already answered. Remember to offer praise before making requests. That being said, also be courageous in your asking. His faithfulness is proof of His promises and blessings all packaged in one. Make your quiet time a real gift for your day.

~

*W*hy not have a Christmas tea party sleep-over? Invite your children's best friends or your grandchildren. Do you need a New Year's Eve party idea for the young children at your house? Slumber parties are always fun.

Before you have tea, go for a drive around the neighborhood and look at all the holiday lights. Everyone can even wear their pajamas for this trip. Or bundle up and walk up and down your block.

Now it's time to get inside, warm up, and get ready for tea and treats. Prepare some cookie dough and let the kids have a cookie-making party. They're great to serve with your tea. And while you're having tea, let each child thank God for something special in his or her life.

~

*D*o you have a guest book? I love reading them. It's the "nosy Emilie" in me, I guess. But it's such an inviting part of being a guest in someone's home. So why not get a guest book and put it on a stand near the door or close to an entryway wall you've dedicated to family and friends' pictures?

~

*D*o you set life goals? Paul says, "I press on to take hold of that for which Christ Jesus took hold of me…I do not consider myself yet to have taken hold of it. But one thing I do: Forgetting what is behind and straining toward what is ahead, I press on toward the goal to win the prize for which God has called me heavenward in Christ Jesus" (Philippians 3:12-14). If you don't have a target, you'll never know if you've hit or missed it. Goal setting can take hard work and, yes, some personal sacrifice, but the alternative is confusion and lack of momentum. There's nothing like devoting time, energy, and sacrifice to your goals because the success you'll experience is delightful. Make prayer one of your goals. And Bible study. And don't forget memorizing Scripture. Press on!

*R*eady for a little quiz? Give yourself one point for every "yes" answer.

- Do you feel you don't have enough space in your home?

- Are things piling up in the closet?

- Are there stacks of unread magazines sitting around?

- Do certain items constantly get lost?

- Are items collecting on the top of the refrigerator?

- Are you finding stuff you haven't used in over a year?

- Are you buying things you already have because you can't find them?

If your score is 0 to 3, you're doing really well. If your score is 4 to 7, you could use some improvement. With a little organization your life could be so much simpler and you'd have more time for God, family, and friends.

o you spend enough time with your hubby? Why not get out your calendars and set aside a couple of nights for dates? Really, you can't afford not to. And once the dates are set, protect those times. Don't let anything interfere. I know you want to make sure all the bases are covered, that nothing's left undone, but you may have to set aside some of your other goals to make time for the important people in your life—your family, other loved ones, friends, your quiet time with the Lord.

~

*H*ave you ever done a "prayer walk"? You'll love the results. Plan to take about 45 minutes. Start by having a 15-minute quiet time in God's Word. Then begin your walk. Adore God and praise Him as you move along. If you spot someone, say a silent prayer for that person—asking God to bless his or her life. Take in the scenery around you. Enjoy the flowers, the grass, the animals. Praise God for the opportunities He gives you to reach out to others. Thank Him for His forgiveness, His faithfulness, the way He helps you when you're tired and overwhelmed. Ask Him to bring to your heart the names on your prayer list...and anyone else who could use special prayer at that time. I guarantee this won't be your last "prayer walk."

~

*L*et me encourage you today. I want to say, "Take some time for yourself!" Here are a few simple ideas to get you started.

- Call your local spa and sign up for a manicure or a pedicure. It'll do wonders for you!

- Do a prayer walk.

- Start reading a great book.

- Get together with a friend for lunch.

- Buy flowers just for you.

- Spend time with a friend who could use someone right now.

- Read some of the biblical psalms.

- Memorize a Bible verse.

Over the years, God has taught me to put "first things first," and sometimes that means *me*. Learn to *care* for yourself. How else will you be able to care for others?

*W*e're reminded in Scripture to "be content whatever the circumstances" (Philippians 4:11). Sometimes that's easier said than done. When

Every Woman Should Know

we're overwhelmed, it's often difficult to experience contentment. One thing that helps me is to establish goals. I ask, "Where am I going? What do I need to get there? Will this save me time? Will this activity improve my walk with the Lord?" The answers to these and other questions help me prioritize.

*W*ant a few different ideas for spending quality time with friends? One idea I heard about involves cleaning out closets. Before you groan too loudly, there's more to this. The two friends who did this organized three baskets. One for charity, one for trash, and one for items that go back into closets. Then they got to work…and had a lot of fun doing it together.

Another idea is to dump all those photos you've both accumulated on your kitchen table (in separate piles). Start organizing them for a family memory book or for special "family and friends" CDs. This is a great time for talking about the great times with your kids, your marriages, your friends, and best of all, your walk with the Lord. Start your own "Project Friendship."

203

What kind of a listener are you? This skill doesn't come easy for most of us...It sure doesn't for me, anyway. But like a lot of other things, listening can be mastered if we practice. The next time you interact with a person or in a crowd, observe how you speak and listen. And if you're really brave, ask a friend to gently evaluate your listening skills. You'll need a loving and willing spirit to hear the critique, but you'll benefit in the long run...as will your family and friends. James 1:19 is a great reminder: "Everyone should be quick to listen, slow to speak and slow to become angry."

~

Life can be hectic. The good news is that God didn't create you for confusion and disorder. In fact, the Bible tells us a thankful heart is a happy heart. When you're grateful for what you have, you enjoy life a lot more...and the people around you enjoy you a lot more.

~

Christmas is one of my favorite times of the year. The company of friends and family, homes beautifully decorated, gifts carefully wrapped and under the tree. And when you celebrate the greatest gift of all—the coming of Jesus—the spirit of the season is even more contagious.

~

*I*sn't it about time for some good old-fashioned spring cleaning? I'm not talking about closets and garages...at least not today. I'm talking about getting rid of some of the clutter in your life so there's more time for God. Just 15 minutes a day can make a big difference. Praying and spending time in the Word...when was the last time you did that? Set aside time today!

~

*O*rganized." If just the word makes you cringe, then listen up. It might surprise you to know that 85 percent of stress is caused by disorganization. That's why so many "organization" TV shows and books are so popular. The benefits to having order in your life include relieved stress, hours redeemed, relaxation, and more time for fun. So get rid of stuff you don't use. A friend of mine confessed to filling four giant plastic bags with nothing but clothes she no longer wears. What can you toss or recycle or give away this week?

~

*I*t's time to rebuild your dream house. No, I'm not talking about where you live, but how you live. As a godly woman, you're the mortar that holds together your home and family. God's Word says homes are made by wisdom. The flip side is that homes can be destroyed by foolishness. Ask God for directions on what you can do to make the situation you're in a better one—whether financially or otherwise. Did you know that nearly 90 percent of new businesses are started by women working out of their homes? God, family, and career. When everything's in God's placement, there will be success.

⁓

A great woman is willing to make positive changes. Are you facing a difficult situation? A troubled marriage, a hard relationship, a not-so-stable job? What can you do to make it better? The answer is wrapped up in a hard word for most humans: "submission." Submission to God, that is. Give Him your family, your spouse, your marriage, your job, and you. He can change the people involved, the situation, or even you. Give Him your attitudes, your behaviors, your stress, your career—all the areas where you need peace. Make prayer a priority, read your Bible, attend church, and have a teachable spirit. You'll be a liberated woman in Jesus Christ. He's your source of strength, love, forgiveness, peace, and joy.

~

*T*here's nothing more fun or more satisfying than making your home you. The frustrating part is paying for it. So why not window-shop the expensive stores to get decorating ideas, and then go to more economical places and shop for the best bargains and alternatives to get a similar look? Another great way to see what's new is to visit model homes or go on "tours of homes" that are offered annually in many areas. "Style isn't what you have, it's what you do with what you have." That's true in so many areas. God has "decorated"…or gifted you…in unique ways. He's looking to you to make the most of His wonderful gifts.

~

*W*hy not go somewhere or do something you've never done before? Branch out and take that risk. Cook up a new recipe, go on a missions trip, learn a new language, cultivate a new friend, volunteer in a new area, throw a block party for your neighbors. We humans get into ruts so easily, and when we do our world can get humdrum. I encourage you to look forward to something! Jesus came to bring us abundant life, and isn't that worth getting excited about?

～

I have an assignment for you. Ready? Write down six things you like about yourself. Did I just hear a groan? An "Oh no!"? Don't be scared. Are you a woman who prays? That's wonderful! Write it down: "I like that I'm a woman of prayer." Do you take care of your family? That's another one: "I like that I take care of my family." Have you encouraged a friend in the past week? "I like that I'm a person who is an encourager to others." When you baked those cookies, made those beds, drove the kids to soccer practice, did you realize what a great gal you were being? Six things you like about yourself is a great exercise. And then thank God for helping you and giving you those gifts!

～

I still struggle with priorities sometimes. Do you? As moms, children sometimes rank at the top of our priorities, but should they be at the pinnacle? Yes, God has given you kiddos as a gift. And He's going to help you (and your husband) take care of them. But it won't be long before they're out of the nest and creating families of their own. And then you and your husband will be left alone. If you haven't worked on your relationship, this new era is going to be very difficult. So make sure your priorities are correct: God, husband, and children.

ith a friend, I'm never too fat, too thin, or too old. Isn't that a relief? Friends can be your lifeline, your sanity saver. And you know what? You keep those friendships alive by little acts of faithfulness:

- showing up for your coffee date

- thinking twice before canceling your walk together

- praying for her

- sending notes of encouragement

- sending "thinking of you" cards just for fun

Most of the time a little everyday maintenance is

all you need—a phone call, an e-mail, a quick visit, and a promise to get together again soon. I've gotta go for now...there are a couple of calls I want to make.

~

I have a few home decorating tips to share today. Do you wonder what to do with blank walls? Hang paintings, prints, and photographs. And they don't have to be expensive. Look for items that express a part of who you are...your interests. I know a sports fan who decorated his office walls with sports magazine covers in box frames. My favorite idea is creating a wall filled with photos of people you love. Another idea is an arrangement of calendar prints that remind you of places you've traveled. Have fun making your home interesting and inviting.

~

*A*re you a collector? That's great! Hmmm... let me clarify: "Stashing" and "piling" is *not* a good thing. There's more to collecting than just accumulating items. Collections help us organize our lives by assigning meaning to what I call "miscellaneous experiences." My collections are important to me because they're chosen for a reason. I've assigned

Every Woman Should Know

to each item a meaning…a memory. And collecting invites conversation, promotes storytelling, and creates personal connections. It draws others in for times of sharing the things we value and care about.

If only there were more hours in the day! Do you relate to that cry? As a woman I'm sure you're already multitasking. It's the perfect answer to needing more time. Another tip is to get your to-do list going and stick to it. Even rank the items by priority to help you get the essentials done. Avoid interruptions if you can, and that means staying away from e-mails and other distractions until your projects are completed. I read somewhere that most people are interrupted at least once every five minutes. If you're the mom of young children, you can make that once every other minute! Take control of your time. With a little practice you might even have time for a quiet moment with a cup of tea.

Put togetherness back into your family. A difficult but very effective way to garner more unity is to schedule two nights a week with no TV. Too hard?

Try one night then. Use the time to be in the same
room reading (everyone can read his or her own book),
talking, playing, putting puzzles together. Or maybe
establish special date nights for you and each of your
children. And when's the last time you and your husband had a night to yourselves? Don't neglect creating
moments to strengthen your family relationships.

~

*A*h, stress! We all have it, so the trick is to
manage it. Sometimes it boils down to good,
old-fashioned planning ahead.

- Why not color-code your extension cords
  when you have several at one outlet?

- Sew extra buttons for your clothing on
  the inside or at the bottom hem. No more
  searching for just the right button.

- Tape the extra screws that come with furniture to the underside of them.

- Refill your car's gas tank before it's on empty.

~

*Y*es, there are times when I don't take the time
to be with the Lord in prayer. I know He loves

me anyway, but I also know that I'm really missing out. In Luke 18:1, Jesus said we ought to pray always, without giving up. Prayer doesn't have to be an organized, regimented activity. Simply open your heart to God. Praise Him for who He is and what He's given to you. Then confess your shortcomings and share how much you trust Him to help you. God hears you! (And nobody else needs to know what you share with Him.)

~

Today I have a few *big* ideas to share. If you walk into my friend Robin's house, your eye goes immediately to a huge and beautiful armoire. She's learned a simple yet effective decorating trick: focusing attention on one large item. Do you have a piano, a fireplace, a wrap-around sofa? If the piano reflects your love of music, why not emphasize that aspect of your room? Frame an old piece of sheet music, hang old instruments, and include photos of favorite musicians. By all means don't let that oversized TV screen be the focus of a room…unless it's in a den or family room used for TV watching.

~

*R*eady for a garage sale? Experts say the fastest-selling items are furniture. Chests of drawers in particular. Then, surprisingly, come dish sets and flower arrangements. Baby items and electronics are next, along with old parts people can use to repair items they already have. Sporting goods always sell big as well. One sure-fire idea is a "bargain bin" filled with anything you want to sell quickly. And why not have a free box that has some worthwhile-but-inexpensive items as a crowd draw? The idea is to get rid of some of the junk (oops—I mean wonderful quality items!) you have lying around.

*W*hat are your goals? You don't have any? Or you only have the goal to "get through today"? Why not make a list of 10 goals you'd like to achieve by the end of this year? Some may be as simple as getting on a schedule. You're more than capable of handling your appointments, money, clothing, I'm positive. And I guarantee that once you get into the spiritual disciplines of prayer and Bible study, that discipline will carry over into other areas too. What are you waiting for? Get started today!

*H*ave you thought about bringing the outdoors in? Decorate with flowers! Anything that holds water can be used for a fresh bouquet. Old drinking glasses, teapots, vintage bottles—a simple arrangement is always the best. Two long-stemmed flowers in a bud vase can be elegant. So can a single blossom floating in a bowl. Or lay your flowers right on the table for a stunning centerpiece. You can tie them in bunches with ribbon or wind them around candles. Use your imagination. God has given us incredible plants to enjoy. And what a wonderful reminder to praise the Creator who made beauty possible.

*H*ow often have you thought, *I'd love to have that, but I'm afraid to ask God. Besides, I'm just being selfish.* I assure you, God wants to hear the desires of your heart. His concern isn't the things you want…it's your attitude about the items. So when you ask, make sure you go with His priorities: "Lord, I'd really like to have this item, but if it would harm me or interfere with my walk with You…or someone else's walk with You, then I really don't want it. If You do give it to me, I'll be very grateful and use it for Your glory." And remember to thank God for *all* things: "Sing and make music in your heart to the Lord, always giving thanks to God the Father for everything, in the name of our Lord Jesus Christ" (Ephesians 5:19-20).

~

*D*evote yourself to prayer, and keep alert with an attitude of thanksgiving. That's the wonderful call to prayer we get from Colossians 4:2. Do you wonder what to pray for? Here are some reminders that work for me:

- Let God know you adore Him.

- Confess your sin to Him.

- Thank Him.

- Make a list of the needs of your family, your children, your friends.

- Pray for friends, your pastor and his family, your country, and missionaries.

When is the *best* time to pray? Morning, noon, and night! God is always ready to listen.

~

*A*re you someone who just can't pass up a good deal? Well today I've got four principles to help you manage your money. First, recognize God owns everything—your home, your car, your children, your talents. Second, to have financial freedom your income has to exceed your expenses. Pretty simple, but that's where we tend to get into trouble. Third, if your spiritual purpose is to serve God, all of your resources minister to that end. And fourth, regularly give money to the Lord—lovingly and obediently, no matter what the amount is. God will use it to minister to others, and you will receive a blessing in return.

*W*hen space is at a premium we need to work smart. Why not remodel an antique armoire and put your entertainment center inside? Use boxes. They make great storage, and you can stack them just about anywhere. Use the tops of cabinets and hutches to creatively store flower arrangements or any attractive item. Luggage you're not using is ideal storage. Oh, by the way, throwing out or giving away things you no longer use also works.

*I*f you're rushing around and getting absolutely nothing accomplished, here's some advice for you: *Stop!* God's Word says, "The LORD has done what he planned; he has fulfilled his word" (Lamentations 2:17). But when you're constantly in a rush you don't have time to think about the really important issues in life. You need some quiet time to think… and pray…and study your Bible. Someone once said, "Hectic lives don't permit one to hear the heartbeat of the soul." You need time for yourself or your personal growth will come to a standstill. Ask, "How do I really want to live my life?" Begin right now to act on your answer.

*N*eed some rainy-day fun things to do with children? All you need is some construction paper, glue, and a little imagination! You'll be making personal placemats for all the members of your family. Cut the paper to the size you want, and then have the kids decorate with handprints, photos, drawings—whatever they like. It's so much fun to see what they come up with. Once their masterpieces are done, have them laminated at a local copy shop. Now you have wonderful conversation pieces for your table setting. And these make great gifts for grandmas and grandpas, aunts and uncles.

~

*A*lmost every woman I know loves a day shopping with a friend. Even if you don't buy anything, the main point is to enjoy laughing, looking, feeling, and trying on clothes together. "Look at this!" "Oh, this is great!" "Hey, I'll bet you could make this one!" Sound familiar? Then after a couple of hours have tea at an elegant department-store tea room or coffee at a quiet coffeehouse. Frankly, our friends are lifelines and sanity savers. We need them to grow and be strong. First Peter 4:10 says, "Each one should use whatever gift he has received to serve others, faithfully administering God's grace in its various forms." Get started today!

~

*I*n the good old days... Does anyone actually remember when that was? Well, in those so-called "good old days," the family had to pitch in to get all the chores done around the farm. Often parents and children worked side by side. While they did, they talked about politics, values, morals, Sunday school lessons, and myriad other things. Today we have to plan time to talk together because we're so busy. Use every opportunity you can to teach your children; casual moments are usually the very best times. They're what I call "memory moments"...times when your children grasp important concepts that will stay with them all their lives.

᠆᠆᠆

*W*hen was the last time you had a "saved for my family" day? The Bible says there's an appointed time for everything, and there's a time for every event under heaven (Ecclesiastes). As I've grown wiser, I realize there are precious times I need to protect. Time with my husband and family. We may not go anywhere or do anything out of the ordinary, but together it's "special time." We can do anything we want: sleep in, stay out late, go to lunch, read a book. When you control your calendar, life is more enjoyable. And the tensions of a busy lifestyle are better managed. Recharge your relationships by spending time together.

᠆᠆᠆

For more information on Emilie's books, seminars, products, and materials from More Hours in My Day Seminars, visit:

www.EmilieBarnes.com

e-mail Emilie at:

emilie@emiliebarnes.com

or send a self-addressed, stamped envelope to:

More Hours in My Day
2150 Whitestone Dr.
Riverside, CA 92506